Inspiring People At Work

How To Make Participative Management Work For You

Thomas L. Quick

 Executive Enterprises Publications Co., Inc.

ISBN 0-88057-402-X
Library of Congress Catalog Card No. 85-080671

About the Author

Thomas L. Quick is executive director of Resource Strategies Institute and supervises the publication of its two monthly newsletters, *Professional Managing* and *Professional Selling*. For twenty-one years, he was a member of the professional staff of the Research Institute of America, where, as managing and then directing editor, he was responsible for the production of sales, supervisory, and management memberships publications.

He has been involved in the training and development field for twenty-five years. At the present time he serves as director of Region One of the American Society for Training and Development. As a management and training consultant, he specializes in motivation and productivity, management methods, and leadership skills.

Tom Quick has written twelve other books, chiefly on management, three of which have been published by Executive Enterprises Publications Co., Inc.: *Understanding People at Work, Managing People at Work Desk Guide,* and *Increasing Your Sales Success.*

Table of Contents

Introduction

The late Rensis Likert has been called the "father" of participative management. Likert, a social scientist who was director of the Institute for Social Research at the University of Michigan, set forth his thinking and research in the books *New Patterns of Management* (1961) and *The Human Organization* (1967), both published by McGraw-Hill. Likert defined participative management as a system in which people who will be affected by a decision are invited to share in the decision-making process. They are given a real voice, a chance to contribute ideas, to evaluate those of others, to help shape the outcome of the deliberations.

It was Likert's conviction that not only do better decisions come out of participation, but that people are more highly committed to carrying them out. Involvement in a decision or action that affects them gives employees a sense that they have some

power over their destiny; that they can develop ways to realize their personal goals in working for the organization.

Likert categorized organizations into four systems:

System 1—Exploitative authoritative. Management does not trust subordinates. Subordinates are not free to discuss matters with supervisors, nor are their opinions sought in solving problems. Motivation comes from fear, threats, and occasional rewards. Communication chiefly comes down from higher management. The information that goes up tends to be inaccurate. Goals are ordered from on high, where all the decisions are made. The informal groups in the organization tend to exist in opposition to the wishes of higher management.

System 2—Benevolent authoritative. Management and employees exist in a master-servant relation-

1

ship. There is some involvement of employees, more rewards than in System 1, slightly better upward communication. This is a paternalistic organization, not unfriendly, as is System 1, but without much employee satisfaction.

System 3—Consultative. Management keeps control of things, but employees are consulted before solutions to problems and decisions are made by management. Communication upward is better, but it is still cautious. Unpleasant or unfavorable information is not offered freely. Employees have the feeling they will perform some roles in preliminary stages of decision-making and policy-setting, but that their contributions may not be taken seriously all the time. Informal groups may go along with the formal organization or exist in opposition to management policies.

System 4—Participative group. Management trusts employees, regards them as willingly working toward the achievement of organizational objectives. People are motivated by rewards. At all levels, they are involved in discussing and deciding those issues that are important to them. Communication is quite accurate and goes up, down, and across. Goals are not ordered from on high, but are set with the participation of the people who will have to work to achieve them. Informal organizations are benign; they support the formal organization.

The most productive organization in Likert's view is the participative group. In this kind of organization, decisions are better because the people who know the most about the issues join together in deciding. This is in contrast to the organization in which, say, marketing decisions are made not by marketers, but by executives at the top, who may be trained in finance or the law.

Because the flow of information is up, down, and across, communications throughout are more effective in transmitting what the organization needs to know in order to function. Not only are the lines and the transmission more complete than in the hierarchy in which the lines are vertical, but also the information is more accurate. Management trusts those down the line and does not feel that letting go of data is tantamount to surrendering power and status. People on lower levels know how important it is that management be apprised of what is going on; they feel less hesitant to let management know **all** the facts, not just the better-sounding ones. Motivation is stronger because rewards are based on the quantity and quality of employee participation.

There are three basic concepts of System 4:

1. The manager's use of the principle of supportive relationships;
2. The manager's use of group decision-making and group methods of supervision; and
3. High performance goals for the organization.

What is supportive is basically ego-building. The employee's interactions with others increase and maintain his or her sense of personal worth. Bosses and peers seek the employee's expertise, listen to him or her, and value the contribution.

The System 4 organization sets objectives that, to the extent possible, reflect the needs and desires of employees, shareholders, customers, suppliers, and others who deal with it. Everyone benefits. Everyone is provided for, valued and looked out for. The needs of the employees to achieve their personal goals and to grow in the job are especially important.

Likert maintained that managers view System 4 as the one in which they believe they can operate more effectively. To confirm this, he conducted research using what has become known as the Likert Instrument—forty-three operating characteristics arranged in an evaluation form. Managers were asked to rate organizational variables in terms of how effective they seem in motivating worker productivity. Their choices of "most productive," "least productive," etc., are marked on a line representing a scale of effectiveness.

One variable might list "fear" at the extreme left of the horizontal line in dealing with the way to run an organization. "Compensation and participation" might be at the right end of that line. According to Likert, most managers marked the left-hand characteristics as "least productive"; the right-hand listings as "most productive." The left side corresponds to System 1; the right side, to System 4.

Perhaps the greatest testimony to Rensis Likert has come from the Japanese, who have enthusiastically adopted the principles of the participative group system—with results that are well known.

Likert's research, of course, did not take place in a vacuum. For thirty years evidence had been mounting that supported the organization's need to place a higher value on their people resources; that there was a definite cause-and-effect relationship between placing that higher value and increasing productivity.

The Hawthorne experiments were probably the first to establish that working conditions could affect productivity. The experiments were conducted at the Hawthorne plant of Western Electric Company in the late 1920's and 1930's. In some of the experiments, productivity went up, apparently as a result of employees being given greater freedom over their work and decreased supervision.

Perhaps the most significant discovery of the studies was the influence of the informal groups they encountered among employees.

How each employee felt about the work and the company was to a large extent determined by the employee's relationships with others. Employees formed social groups, and these groups could be supportive of organizational policies or obstructive.

Today, we are not as naïve as the Hawthorne management, which apparently didn't know of the existence of such informal groups. These groups satisfy a social need in people by giving them a sense of belonging. The formal organization may not provide that satisfaction. The group may be predominantly social in nature. But it may also hold and enforce values and norms that go against those of the formal organization.

Likert's research defined the roles of the informal groups in each System. In System 1, you'll recall, the groups are in opposition to higher management. The obstructive, defensive roles of the informal group decline as management moves toward the more participative style. In System 4, groups tend to be supportive of management, in part because management includes employees in the management process.

The Hawthorne studies, significant though they were, aroused little attention in the America of the Depression. But after the war, the work of Abraham H. Maslow attracted much notice. Maslow, a professor of psychology at Brandeis University and, later, president of the American Psychological Association, became famous for his Hierarchy of Needs. People are motivated, according to Maslow, to satisfy certain needs ranging from the very basic and bodily to the very complex and psychological. It was Maslow's belief that as you satisfied one level of need, you moved to the next higher one. Starting with the *physiological* —food, sex, drink, and sleep, you moved up the hierarchy to *safety*— security, structure, and order— through *belongingness and love* and *esteem* to *self-actualization*, growing to become what one is capable of being, realizing one's potential.

The notion that people's behavior is directed toward goals or needs wasn't new to psychologists, but it did seem to be novel to laypeople. In the 1960's, everyone began to talk about the Hierarchy—and their place in it. People saw a relationship between what Maslow was saying and how people behave at work. If every action is motivated by a need or directed to a goal, what does that mean on the job? Motivation of people at work was a subject that people began to think about seriously. Furthermore, the thought that people might actually use their work to develop their potential, to fulfill themselves, seemed quite startling. It dawned on some that the traditional ways of looking at people on the job might be suspect. Perhaps work wasn't a punishment that had resulted from expulsion from the Garden of Eden!

Some of the traditional ways of looking at people at work were described by Douglas McGregor, a professor at Massachusetts Institute of Technology and a psychologist who was heavily influenced by Maslow. McGregor became known for his

Theory X and Theory Y. Theory X was the traditional view: People really don't want to work. To get work out of them, management must threaten and coerce them. Actually, Theory X holds, people prefer to be directed. They avoid responsibility, have little ambition, and really value security above all.

But Theory Y is a more contemporary way of looking at people, McGregor suggested: Work is natural to people. They will commit themselves to objectives that provide worthwhile rewards. They not only accept responsibility, they seek it. Finally, the capacity to exercise a relatively high degree of imagination, ingenuity, and creativity in the solution of organizational problems is widely, not narrowly, distributed in the population.

The Theory X–Theory Y distinctions became enormously popular. Suddenly, no manager wanted to admit he or she had Theory X assumptions about people, although it is probable that many did. What they were saying is that *they* fit the Theory Y descriptions. But it's questionable whether many managers accepted that last point about people having ingenuity, imagination, and creativity. Many managers were hardly tapping their people resources, probably because they doubted that subordinates really did have those qualities.

Maslow had suggested that people have needs, and that they work to satisfy those personal needs. McGregor took motivation theory further and said that people will work *in a job* to achieve objectives to which they are committed. It takes only a short jump to assume that people can identify with the goals of an organization. People can achieve personal rewards through fulfillment of organizational objectives.

The importance of Theory X and Theory Y is that stating the theory gave form to certain perspectives that had been in existence but had never before been articulated as scientific theory. Also, McGregor made it respectable to think in terms of people achieving personal objectives through their efforts to help organizations achieve theirs. The work itself could, therefore, be a motivator.

It was Frederick Herzberg who, in the late 1950's, confirmed that work is, indeed, a motivator. Herzberg, a social scientist who was on the faculties of first Carnegie Institute of Technology, and then Case-Western Reserve, and subsequently the University of Utah, published the results of his research in motivation in the book, *The Motivation to Work* (1959). These results became known as the two-factor theory of motivation. According to Herzberg, there are six satisfiers or motivators:

- **Achievement:** The successful completion of a job or a task; a solution; the results of one's work.
- **Recognition of achievement:** An act of praise or some other reward that takes notice of the achievement.
- **Work itself:** The extent of duties and responsibilities.
- **Responsibility:** For one's own work or that of others; new tasks and assignments.
- **Advancement:** An improvement in status or position.
- **Possibility for growth:** Potential to rise in the organization.

That the thinking of Maslow, McGregor, and Herzberg follows parallel paths is immediately recognizable. People are motivated by higher-order needs, such as esteem and self-actualization. They seek responsibility. They want to grow in the work. They seek rewards for their investment of themselves on the job.

Herzberg's research also defined factors that are labeled **dissatisfiers.** Their presence does not motivate; their absence creates dissatisfaction. For example:

- **Supervision:** Its quality is determined by willingness or unwillingness to teach or to delegate responsibility; differences in leadership can result in things running smoothly or being irritating.
- **Company policy and administration:** Structure; good or bad communications; adequate or inadequate authority; harmful or beneficial effects of company and personnel policies.
- **Positive working conditions:** Environmental and physical conditions.
- **Interpersonal relations with peers, subordinates, and bosses:** The social and working transactions with others on the job.
- **Status:** How one's position is perceived by others; perquisites of rank.
- **Job security:** Stability; tenure.
- **Salary:** Compensation.
- **Personal life:** How aspects of the work—such as long hours, or required transfer and relocation—affect the employee's personal life.

But aren't people motivated to achieve money and status? Is Herzberg saying that these are not motivators? The answer is that people on the job can be motivated to achieve status and more money. Once achieved, however, the status and money no longer motivate. And if people believe they do not have the status and money they deserve, they are dissatisfied. The same is probably true of surroundings. The thought of achieving a better physical working environment through good performance is a motivator. But employees who already work in a nice environment do not feel a motivating pull from that factor.

Another question involves the relationship between dissatisfiers and demotivation. Can employees who are dissatisfied experience demotivation? In Herzberg's language, a satisfier is a motivator. It's probably true that a similar relationship exists between dissatisfaction and demotivation. Interestingly, the managers who formed the basis of Rensis Likert's research believe there is such a relationship. Many of the dissatisfiers appear on the left hand of the scale, whereas the majority of the managers surveyed believed that the factors contributing to productivity are on the right hand of the scale (System 4), where the satisfiers appear.

The contributions of Maslow and McGregor were innovative and seminal, even if they were largely conceptual and theoretical. They were also timely. In the economic climate of the 1950's and 1960's, there was a need for a new way of looking at people at work. Many people found the theories personally useful in identifying their own motivators. To some extent, the almost universal acceptance of both Maslow's and McGregor's theories provides some validation for them. More scientific validation is provided by the research conducted by Herzberg and Likert, although in the beginning Herzberg was criticized as having used too narrow a population base for his work. But in the twenty-five years following publication, most people believe that Herzberg's conclusions have been amply validated and supported by organizations that have applied his theories.

There is also support in the expectancy theory of Victor Vroom of Yale University and in Julian Rotter's social learning theory, both explaining that people are motivated by (a) the reward that they perceive will be theirs as a result of their behavior; and (b) their ability to gain the reward. People choose what is valuable to them so long as they believe they have a reasonable chance to achieve it.

The bulk of the research into the motivation of people on the job has been conducted in the United States. As you can see, there has been a direction to the research, leading to parallel conclusions. Many of the theories have been applied successfully in Japan and Europe; although, unquestionably, participative management/shared leadership is being adopted now by American management. No longer does anyone seriously doubt that it is a valid, worthwhile, and productive direction for any management to take.

Your Organizational Profile

Circle the number on the following scales that, in your opinion, most accurately represents the behavior and atmosphere in the organization of which you and your department are a part.

Management regularly tries to involve employees in decision-making that involves them, or at least solicits and considers information from the lower echelons.			Objectives and decisions originate at the top, generally without input or influence from outside top management.	
5	4	3	2	1

Both management and employees feel that they are members of a unified team.			There is, especially among employees, a feeling of Us vs. Them when it comes to perceptions of management.	
5	4	3	2	1

There is a fairly wide-open flow of information, up and down, through formal channels of communication.			Management seems to regard information as their special province and lets out only what is absolutely necessary.	
5	4	3	2	1

Employees are accepting of management's policies and decisions.			Employees tend to react to management's policies with "What're they doing to us now?"	
5	4	3	2	1

Management regards employees as partners and resources.			Management tends to believe employees are not interested in the organization's well-being.	
5	4	3	2	1

Management encourages and reinforces a steady flow of accurate information from below.			Management seems not interested in receiving information from lower levels, and discourages it.	
5	4	3	2	1

Advancement is based on performance, ability, and commitment.		Advancement seems based on cronyism and politics.	
5 4	3	2	1

The respective perceptions of management and employees of how the organization is functioning and of its effectiveness are fairly close.

There is a wide gap in how management and employees perceive the organization's functioning and effectiveness.

5	4	3	2	1

Management is responsive to and appreciative of unfavorable information from below.

Management's response to unfavorable information from below is, "Employees don't know enough about the operation." Therefore, managers discount the information.

5	4	3	2	1

The long-term development of people ranks as high in priority as short-term performance results.

High priority is given to short-term performance results; low priority is given to long-term development of people.

5	4	3	2	1

Conflict is viewed as normal in a healthy, vibrant organization, and people who manage it well are rewarded.

Conflict is viewed as disruptive and, therefore, suppressed. People involved in conflict may be "punished."

5	4	3	2	1

In meetings, participants are encouraged to share leadership and make consensus decisions.

Meetings are characterized by rigid agendas and/or by power groups that seek to dominate the decision-making.

5	4	3	2	1

Criticism is given by management and seen by employees as an effort to correct performance deficiencies and to increase effectiveness.

People tend to be resentful when they are criticized.

5	4	3	2	1

Feedback is balanced—positive for good performance, negative for faulty performance.		Employees generally receive criticism when they make mistakes, but seldom hear praise when they work well.	
5	4	3	2	1

People look at increased responsibility as both a reward for good performance and as a means to grow and advance.

People view increased responsibility as an imposition, certainly something not to be sought.

| 5 | 4 | 3 | 2 | 1 |

Management style is open and participative.

Management style is predominantly directive and autocratic. Participative managers are viewed with distrust by higher management.

| 5 | 4 | 3 | 2 | 1 |

Both monetary and nonmonetary rewards are used regularly and consistently to recognize and encourage repetition of effective performance.

Management uses the threat of disciplinary action as a prod to obtain acceptable performance from employees.

| 5 | 4 | 3 | 2 | 1 |

The power base is chiefly a mixture of competence and influencing skills.

The source of power is twofold: the position one holds and whom one knows.

| 5 | 4 | 3 | 2 | 1 |

The grapevine generally supplements but does not contradict the formal communication channels.

The grapevine generally is more accurate and complete than formal communication channels.

| 5 | 4 | 3 | 2 | 1 |

Solving problems is characterized by searching for a desirable alternative.

Solving problems is characterized by pinning blame.

| 5 | 4 | 3 | 2 | 1 |

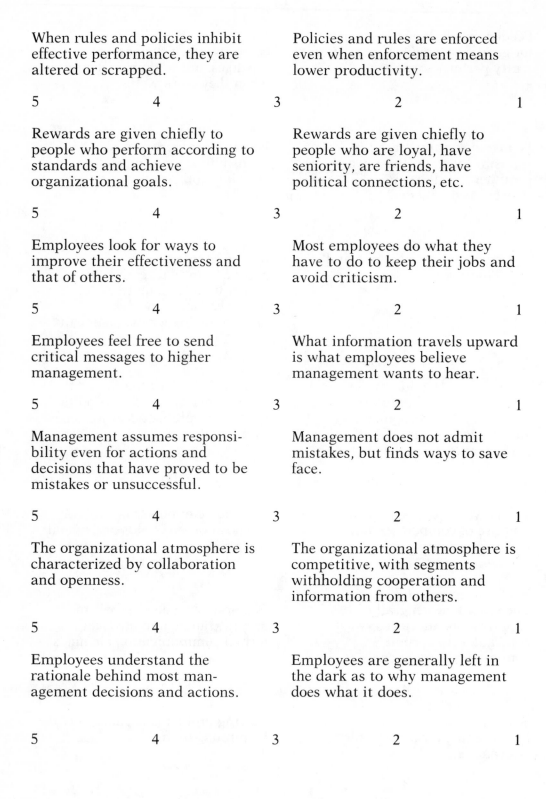

When rules and policies inhibit effective performance, they are altered or scrapped.

Policies and rules are enforced even when enforcement means lower productivity.

5   4   3   2   1

Rewards are given chiefly to people who perform according to standards and achieve organizational goals.

Rewards are given chiefly to people who are loyal, have seniority, are friends, have political connections, etc.

5   4   3   2   1

Employees look for ways to improve their effectiveness and that of others.

Most employees do what they have to do to keep their jobs and avoid criticism.

5   4   3   2   1

Employees feel free to send critical messages to higher management.

What information travels upward is what employees believe management wants to hear.

5   4   3   2   1

Management assumes responsibility even for actions and decisions that have proved to be mistakes or unsuccessful.

Management does not admit mistakes, but finds ways to save face.

5   4   3   2   1

The organizational atmosphere is characterized by collaboration and openness.

The organizational atmosphere is competitive, with segments withholding cooperation and information from others.

5   4   3   2   1

Employees understand the rationale behind most management decisions and actions.

Employees are generally left in the dark as to why management does what it does.

5   4   3   2   1

Management uses persuasion to get acceptance of new rules and policies by employees.

Management introduces new policies and rules with no apparent regard for how employees will view them.

5	4	3	2	1

Absenteeism and turnover are low.

Absenteeism and turnover are high.

5	4	3	2	1

Management assumes that most employees want to do a good job.

Management believes that employees must be monitored or else they will not work well.

5	4	3	2	1

Most employees find meaning and satisfaction in their work.

The attitude of many employees toward the work is that "It's a job."

5	4	3	2	1

Employees and managers take responsibility for their actions, realizing that mistakes will occur.

Employees and managers often look for ways to avoid responsibility and blame.

5	4	3	2	1

In general, employees disapprove of other employees who intentionally bend rules or policies.

Employees wink at other employees who intentionally bend rules and policies or may even take pleasure in infractions.

5	4	3	2	1

Morale is high or satisfactory throughout the organization.

Morale is fairly low throughout the organization.

5	4	3	2	1

Pilfering, thievery, and cheating are seldom encountered.

Employees feel entitled to take what they can from the organization—supplies for personal use, inflated expense accounts, etc.

5	4	3	2	1

Performance evaluations are seen as a means to help employees work more effectively.

Evaluations are suspected of being management's way of controlling employees and justifying disciplinary actions and punishment.

| 5 | 4 | 3 | 2 | 1 |

The emphasis is on sharing authority with high-performing individuals.

Managers tend to guard their authority jealously.

| 5 | 4 | 3 | 2 | 1 |

Management believes that the more people are involved in setting objectives, the more committed they usually are to achieving those objectives.

Objectives are established at the top and mandated downward.

| 5 | 4 | 3 | 2 | 1 |

The free flow of information—up, down, and across—is considered helpful to employees, an indication that they are involved in the well-being of the organization.

Management believes in tightly controlling the flow of information.

| 5 | 4 | 3 | 2 | 1 |

Managers are rewarded for pushing responsibility and decision-making authority downward to high-performing employees and groups.

Managers are criticized for surrendering managerial prerogatives.

| 5 | 4 | 3 | 2 | 1 |

On the preceding forty scales, a score of 200 would indicate an ideal organization, and there are not many of those around. It's probably safe to say that an unfortunately large number of organizations resemble the right end of the scale more closely than the left. The higher the score for your organization, the healthier and more effective it is. The left end of the scale is the profile of an organization with a culture that incorporates many of the features and benefits of participative management/shared leadership.

It's a fair organization, fair in the sense of just and honest. What you see is what is there. A high-scoring organization regards its people as valued resources who are sincerely interested in the well-being of the organization. They are partners. They see their best interests as related to those of the organization. Information flows freely, because, after all, everyone needs to be properly informed and oriented if they are to work effectively. Less pragmatically, as has been stated already, the people are *interested*. They have a natural, healthy curiosity about what is going on. Management has no reason to hide information, as they would if they managed by manipulation and deceit. Information is often referred to as power, and in the participative organization, information/power is shared with all.

That does not mean that all participative organizations are democratic. Not everyone has an equal vote. Not all decisions are voted on. But everyone has the privilege — perhaps even the right — to try to influence a decision. At least, employees have confidence that management will not knowingly and arbitrarily make decisions that are contrary to the welfare of the employees.

In a shared leadership environment, the relationship between management and employees is based on trust, respect, openness, and sharing.

Some managers believe that such openness, trust, sharing, and respect indicate an abdication of management rights and responsibilities. It's a surrender, an easy way out. Quite the contrary. Participative management is difficult to achieve. It takes a long time to build trust and credibility. It's a nurturing process. But the results, sometimes long in coming, are well worth the effort in terms of commitment, motivation, and productivity. People are enthusiastic about coming to work. While there, they look for ways the organization can become even more effective. And they go home feeling good about what they have done.

Chapter One

The Benefits of Participative Management

Why should you want to share your leadership with employees? Many managers don't. Those who have initiated participative management have created a number of benefits for themselves, such as more effectiveness in the work group, better information, higher morale among subordinates, and more satisfaction for themselves. It's worth taking a closer look at the benefits of sharing your leadership.

• **Optimum use of your resources.** In centralized organizations, many employees chafe at the restrictions that are placed upon what they may do. Duties and functions are specifically and, usually, narrowly defined —and often stay the same for long periods of time. Yet people want to have the feeling that they are growing and advancing. Most people want challenge. They do not want sameness and routine. Managers who ease restrictions, who work to enlarge and enrich the jobs of subordinates, are usually surprised and gratified to discover the eagerness with which employees respond. It's not uncommon for employees in a less restrictive environment to look for ways to increase their own effectiveness and that of co-workers. While they need managerial guidance, the results of employees' taking charge of their jobs and responsibilities are generally favorable, if only because they know their jobs and their part of the operation better than their managers do. Since people at work have a natural desire to seek challenge and responsibility, you are going with the grain when you give your subordinates more freedom to do so. You are giving subordinates more opportunities to do what they are capable of doing. You are putting their talents, skills, and knowledge to work in a more efficient manner. You are unleashing their creativity. You'll generally find that, in a participative atmosphere, you have a team of assistants rather than just subordinates.

• **Higher productivity.** When you provide employees with more opportunities to do the kinds of work that they regard as most valuable to them, you can expect greater motivation. People are motivated by the anticipation of achieving rewards from their work. Many of those rewards are internally generated: People want to have a sense of growth, of achievement, or an increase in self-esteem and satisfaction. And they believe they have a better chance to gain the external rewards that you give—money, promotion, praise, etc., because there is a definite link between what people like to do and what they do well. In a decentralized structure, people can choose more of the kinds of tasks and responsibilities that they want to do and will probably do well. Often employees have a better sense of what they can do than their managers. And they certainly know more about what they enjoy doing than their managers. Finally, remember that Herzberg classifies the work itself as a motivator. As you increase the value of that work to the employee, you can expect to see an intensification of the motivating forces in that employee.

• **Better quality.** When people are asked to share the leadership of an operation, when they are given more responsibility, they acquire more ownership. That is, in a participative atmosphere, people are, to use the current expression, given a piece of the action. It is their piece of the action. They own it. They are committed to doing it well because it is theirs. In more centralized organiza-

tions, employees are more concerned with inputs rather than outputs: what they put into the work rather than what comes out of it. But when you share your leadership, you insist that people take responsibility for the *results* of what they do.

• **More complete and accurate information.** Directive managers often suffer from a lack of information about what is going on within and outside their departments. Their subordinates either don't know what is going on, or don't care. Or if they do know, they have no great motivation to share that information with the manager. That's not true in a participative environment. When people have ownership, they have reasons to care about what goes on inside the department that obstructs their effectiveness—other workers, inefficient procedures, unnecessary costs, etc. Also they are concerned with what goes on outside that could affect departmental effectiveness—relationships with other departments, what the grapevine says about the organization, the business environment. If you have twenty employees, you may have twenty sensors responsive to changes and influences. Furthermore, your employees have a vested interest in your receiving accurate information. In many autocratic structures, the information sent up to management is what employees believe management would like to hear rather than what reflects reality. Your people feel responsible, as you do, for the effectiveness of your operation. And that means you must have accuracy as well as information.

• **Improved morale.** While it is true that there is no proven link between motivation/productivity and morale, still, managers legitimately concern themselves with how people feel about their jobs. When morale is high, it's more likely that people will relate better to one another and to higher management. They'll be more open to cooperation and giving support. And they'll be happier. Happier employees don't necessarily produce more, but they do make the work environment more pleasant.

Higher morale usually exists when people feel included and esteemed by management. Morale tends to drop when employees feel left out and unimportant. Obviously, participative management is an including process. Employees become partners with you.

● **Better decisions.** In most operations, employees know more about their work than their managers. Yet many managers will insist on unilateral decision-making that affects employees and their ability to work effectively. Employees' input could contribute to a much better decision, simply because they, as a group, can generate more options and solutions than you can by yourself. In addition, there is much evidence from years of research into group decision-making that consensus results in a decision that is of higher quality than any produced by one person. More heads don't necessarily produce better decisions, but more knowledgeable heads do. Thus it isn't the number of people involved in the process. Rather it's the number of people involved who, collectively, may know more than you do.

Finally, there is the question of ownership. People who participate in producing the decision are more committed to carrying it out than people who have been left out of the process. The decision or solution is, in part, theirs. They have a stake in seeing that it works.

● **An easier, more enjoyable job for you.** When your people willingly travel with you in the direction you wish, when the informal organization in your department supports you and your objectives, your life is a lot easier. You then have more time to do the kinds of work that *only* you can do, or for which you are best suited—budgeting, planning, communicating with other managers or with higher executives, etc. You enjoy the same opportunities you extend to your subordinates: the chance to achieve, to create more satisfaction for yourself from the work you do. While there is no way you can eliminate all the troublesome contingencies, emergencies, and unpleasantries, you can, through sharing your leadership and responsibility, reduce much of the pressure and stress that are barriers to enjoyment.

Countless managers have discovered at least some of these benefits of participative management. Many more, however, resist the notion of sharing their leadership, for one or more of the following reasons:

▼ **They see it as a risk.** And indeed it is. As manager, you delegate some of your authority and responsibility, yet you are still responsible. If you assign an important task to an employee and if that employee fails to complete the task correctly, you can hardly shrug off the fact by pointing the finger at the deficient performance of the employee. **You** are at fault. Regardless of the fact that you delegated, you failed to achieve the required results.

If you have a decision to make, and if you depend on subordinates to help you make it, you could make the wrong choice or take the wrong action if the inputs the subordinates contribute are misleading.

▼ **They don't understand motivation.** Managers who are reluctant to share their power and authority often do not really understand why people behave as they do. Human behavior is based on rewards. People choose to take one course of action over another because the rewards or the results of that action are valuable to them. To manage successfully, a manager would have to understand something of his or her employees' reward preferences—and assign tasks on that basis. It is complicated, but it works. Many managers simply cannot accept that people really are motivated to work, and to work well. Or they don't understand the principles of motivation, which, admittedly, take some thinking through.

▼ **They favor a directive approach.** Once again, some managers prefer what seems to be a simpler, more tidy approach. As is true in the case of understanding motivation, you must keep track of twenty employees, if you have that many, when you delegate. There are twenty different people with twenty sets of skills and aptitudes. To deal successfully with twenty individuals requires a great deal of flexibility. To have twenty "assistants" seems complicated. It is much easier, these managers believe, to treat all twenty the same way. Give orders that apply to all equally. If you ask for input, you may hear one thing from one person, something else from another. If you ask for participation, then you must worry about the concerns of twenty people. The answer, supposedly, is to treat all twenty as one. And further, to restrict much of the communication to one way: from the top, down.

▼ **They have a Theory X perspective.** There are still many managers who believe that most employees really don't want to work or to have responsibility. Thus, if you want to get people to work, you must use fear of punishment. This kind of manager believes that the ultimate reward for doing a good job is being able to keep it. If you give people freedom and responsibility without staying on top of them constantly, they will take advantage of you. They must be controlled and coerced.

▼ **They are elitist.** Some managers regard themselves as special because they are managers. They are a notch above their subordinates. They maintain their distinction in part by keeping distance. Obviously, a more democratic style is not to their liking. You frequently hear such managers suggest that it is not a good managerial policy to socialize with subordinates, as if the familiarity would encourage employees to forget their place.

▼ **They confuse participation with permissiveness.** Participative management does not necessarily reflect the laissez-faire style of management. Depending on the task and the employee, the manager exercises a degree of control. Furthermore, the manager still has the final word, because he or she must answer to higher management. One managing editor held regular editorial meetings with his staff to evaluate the copy they were considering for the publication. The manager's policy was never to publish any article that he had serious objections to, even if all the staff members were in favor of its publication. However, he abided by the majority opinion of the staff in cases of articles which he wanted published, but which they did not. Such managers who share leadership know that they remain ultimately responsible for what happens in their departments; they must retain control to make sure that results are always in accord with their and the organization's objectives.

Participation and delegation are not abdication. Managers who share their power and authority do not give it up. They lend it. They can always take it back. Indeed, they must take it back when they are not getting the results they want; when the work is not being performed up to standards.

▼ **They fear they will be seen as weak and indecisive.** It may be true that other more directive managers will look with disfavor or suspicion on less autocratic approaches to management. What should count—admittedly, it does not always—are the results of the participative style. If a manager can achieve a substantial increase in productivity, he or she ought to be able to ride out the criticism.

▼ **They have no tolerance for ambiguity.** "He's a boss, but he doesn't act 'bossy.'" Some managers don't believe that persuading and influencing are managerial acts. In their minds, you can't be a boss unless you dominate and give orders. The participative approach is more subtle, often more indirect. Managers who practice it may not resemble the traditional role model of the boss. But if they get the desired results, there can't be any question about who runs the show. Managers who share their leadership expertly and successfully may present an ambiguous model to other managers, but not to their employees.

The Qualities of the Participative Manager

It's evident that the successful participative manager is of a different breed from the traditional, more directive manager. How can you measure your disposition toward leadership sharing? The following quiz can help you to determine how successful you can be at managing participatively. The more **yes** answers you can arrive at, the more expert you are, or will be.

1. I frequently look for "stretching" tasks and assignments that will require employees to expand their knowledge and sharpen their skills or acquire new ones.   Y   N

2. Before making a decision that affects employees, I consult with them and seriously consider their opinions and recommendations.   Y   N

3. I regularly solicit information from key subordinates about the department's operations, realism in terms of objectives, emerging problems, etc., and accept that information as sincere, even if it is unfavorable.   Y   N

4. In my meetings, I encourage every member to participate freely and to share leadership with me, even if it means that I must subordinate my position of authority for the time being.   Y   N

5. If employees seem resistant to a change I want to make, I use persuasive and influencing skills rather than ordering compliance.   Y   N

6. I believe in keeping employees fully informed about what is happening in the organization, except when the information I possess is labeled **confidential** by higher management.   Y   N

7. One of my principal pleasures as a manager is helping employees to find ways to increase their effectiveness and satisfaction on the job.   Y   N

Y

N

8. I am convinced that most employees will commit themselves to my and the organizational goals if they believe that by doing so they will achieve job satisfaction and their own objectives.

Y

N

9. A collaborative spirit in my department is much more valuable to me than competitiveness between employees.

Y

N

10. I do not feel less of a manager when I delegate some of my responsibilities, share decision-making with employees, and permit them to devise their own methods for accomplishing tasks, so long as those methods meet my performance standards.

Some Perspectives of the Participative Manager

Much of what you read in the following pages of this book is concerned with how you can effectively share your leadership and get the results you want from your subordinates. It is practical, how-to advice. And it is based on certain attitudes. How you see yourself is essential to the success of your efforts to manage participatively. In general, the following five characteristics constitute a profile of the participative manager:

1. You understand how groups can add to your department's productivity. Many managers do not understand how the successful management of groups within their department can increase employee productivity, and they may even fear that the encouragement of committees, task forces, quality circles, etc., will challenge managerial authority. Groups have personalities,

and as such, they can be subversive. That is, they can resist control.

But the participative manager understands that groups, even though they are entities and not merely aggregates of employees, can increase the resources available to him or her. A good group is synergistic, providing a whole that is greater than the sum of its parts. A decision or a solution generated by consensus is usually of a higher quality than what the brightest and most talented member of the group could produce individually.

Not only do you understand the advantages that a group presents you with, you appreciate that it takes a special set of skills in you to help that group develop effectively. And when you see the benefits to you of that group's development, you cease to be threatened by its existence. Instead, you enjoy the increased quality and quantity of production that a successful problem-solving, decision-making, or advisory body can achieve.

Groups will take on a life of their own. They come together, coalesce, and "die." You must know how to organize them, nurture them, and replace them after they have lived their useful lives.

2. You see yourself as a facilitator and coordinator. Many managers perceive themselves as directors. What gets done, they believe, is the result of a direct action on their part. The facilitator is more indirect. He or she gives the employees power and permission to accomplish a task or an objective, then acts as a guide and resource to ensure its accomplishment. The facilitator thus facilitates rather than directs, making it possible for others to do the work. The manager must also coordinate the work being done by individuals and groups so that the overall departmental objectives are met. The manager acts as both the facilitator and the coordinator when rivalry, conflict, and misunderstandings arise and threaten to disrupt the effectiveness of subordinates. The directive manager sees himself or herself as achieving results through acting *on* people. The facilitator/coordinator gets things done *through* people.

3. You take long-term responsibility for your employees. Whereas many of your managerial colleagues look predominantly for immediate returns on their investments in employees' activities, you feel an obligation to get short-term and long-term results from your management of subordinates. You believe it is shortsighted to neglect the development of your people resources. And it is. The payoff from a continuing development of employees comes both today and tomorrow. In the near term, your helping employees to grow and advance in their responsibilities has a motivational effect. You enable your subordinates to work better, which increases their motivation, and you help them to acquire greater expertise when they have achieved your objectives. They may see your help as a recognition of their achievement, i.e., a reward. Rewards have strong motivational influence, of course.

In the long term, you develop your employees through coaching, training, experience, and education to cope with the changing work environment—in the organization, in the industry, in the laws, in the economy. The skills and knowledge that your people will require tomorrow to do an effective job will be somewhat different from what gets the job done today.

You don't just manage for today, or even just for this quarter. You manage for years to come. And you'll get periodic dividends from your continuing investment.

4. You value respect and credibility above all in your relationships with your subordinates. You want employees to believe that you know what you're doing and that what you tell them is, so far as you know, accurate. You want them to respect you and trust you.

Some managers want to be liked. Others seem to want to be feared. Some value personal loyalty above everything else. And many managers do not appear to respect their subordinates.

But you believe that if you say that you will reward them if they do the job you want, they will accept your word. If you assure them that you will look out for their interests and welfare, they will be convinced that you will. If you promise them that you will do all in your power to help them be effective and gain from their work what is important to them, they will follow your guidance and accept your standards.

But you must also believe that they want to do a good job, that they want to be effective, that, given a decent opportunity, they want to commit themselves to your objectives. You have to extend to them the same understanding you have of yourself: that you are motivated to gain rewards from the work you do. You accept that the people you manage are, psychologically, no different from you in their interest in their jobs. They may have different goals, but they are motivated, as you are, to achieve their objectives through work.

A few years ago, Transactional Analysis defined the relationship between your employees and you very well: I'm okay, you're okay.

It takes a long time for a manager

to be respected and believed by subordinates, which may be the reason why many managers seem to ignore the importance of being respected and believed. But it is unlikely that there can be a successful partnership between manager and subordinates where there is insufficient trust, respect, and credibility—going both ways.

5. You look at information as power, and the more accurate information you have, the more power. The more options you have from which to choose, the more power you have. If you are to increase the options on which you base your planning and decisions, you need all the information you can get. Even as manager, you don't have all the information. Your employees have their own grapevines and perspectives, and you can benefit from getting their opinions and interpretations. If your subordinates are willing to share what they know with you, they will expand your treasury of information substantially. But they must be willing to share, and usually they will be, when they trust you, respect you, want you to succeed. Chances are, they perceive their fortunes to be tied to yours. If the relationship is indeed a partnership, you can expect that they will act in your behalf, gathering, reporting, and interpreting information that can only help you.

Thus it takes a secure person to be a participative manager. In a real sense, to share your leadership puts you at risk. You are, after all, acknowledging your dependence on others to make your job a success. But, at the same time, you recognize that others care about their success, too, and that they depend on you to help them achieve what they need.

The results of such a collaboration often exceed the expectations of everyone involved.

Chapter Two

Communicating for Results

As a manager, you have a right—and an obligation—to communicate to your subordinates what you need and want from them. Your employees have to know what you expect of them in order to work according to your standards and achieve your objectives. They need to know how well they work according to those standards. When they have, or have not, achieved your objectives, they need to know that as well. Thus, if you are to have an effective work group, your communicating with them is vital when you set goals, evaluate performance, correct deficiencies, and recognize achievement.

But *what* you communicate is only one factor. *How* is equally important. You can tell a salesperson that you want more new business calls made, a production worker that you want quotas met regularly, the clerical worker or data processor that you want output increased and mis-

takes decreased, a supervisor that you want more of his or her employees upgraded in their skills. But if, in the telling, you create confusion or resentment, you might as well have saved your words. Resentful employees will give you grudging cooperation, at best, but their feelings toward you and the work could undermine their motivation.

Obviously, your long-term objective is to build a work team that performs in harmony with you in the achievement of organizational—and your—goals. They must involve themselves willingly in the work and commit themselves to achieving those objectives.

Your mode of behavior in communicating has much to do with whether you get poor, barely adequate, good, or even excellent performance from subordinates. Just as important, your communicating is a key to building an effective, closely knit work team for the future.

Taking Control

A major misunderstanding that many managers have of participative management or shared leadership is that it is, in reality, permissive management. Their misconception is that the manager surrenders control to employees. For example, a manager is very concerned, even a bit angry, that one of his key employees seems to be dragging his feet on an important job. The manager believes the job should have been wound up already. Not only has it not, the manager realizes he doesn't even know how far along the employee is toward accomplishing the task. The manager stops by the employee's office and asks about progress. "It's coming along," the employee assures the manager. "We've had some delays, people out sick. Then there was that rush job that caused us to have to put everything else aside for a few days. But we're back on track. I'll be in touch with you, shortly, to bring you up to date."

"Well, all right," the manager replies. "Let me know when you're ready."

This manager has responded in a way that is familiar and very human. He has chosen to be patient, indulgent, understanding when confronted by behavior that he actually finds irritating, even offensive. More correctly, he has chosen to appear to be patient, indulgent, etc. He suppresses his real feelings. The psychologist would say that the manager is *nonassertive.* He will not express himself or state positively that the subordinate is doing something disagreeable—not communicating on the progress of the assignment—and that the employee owes the manager something and is not meeting that obligation.

When people choose to be nonassertive in a situation, they justify it by saying that they don't want to be embarrassed by causing a scene or they don't want to offend someone. It's an avoidance of pain. But when you do not assert yourself, you prevent yourself from getting the kind of behavior you want from others. For a manager, that is a serious deficiency. Furthermore, you encourage the other person to continue behaving in an undesirable or objectionable manner.

In reality, many people have good intentions when they choose to be nonassertive and decline to stand up for their rights. Perhaps because of their upbringing, they are hesitant, or believe it is inappropriate to say to others, "I want you to . . ." or "I need . . ."

For a manager, nonassertiveness is *never* appropriate. You have the right and the obligation to seek what you need and want in the way of acceptable performance from your subordinates.

The opposite of nonassertive behavior is aggressiveness. Some managers practice aggressiveness, routinely. For example, assume that the manager who was nonassertive in the preceeding illustration, chose aggressiveness instead. Here is how the manager's statement might have gone:

"I want you to know that I'm sick and tired of your goofing off. Here I try to be nice, to give you a lot of room to move in, and what do you do? You take advantage of me. Well, I'm onto your game and I'm giving you a warning. If you don't wrap this job up, and wrap it up fast, I'll find someone else who can do it, and you can take your little games somewhere else."

This manager is angry and lets the subordinate know it. He is also aggressive. Some people confuse aggressiveness with being assertive. But the two modes of behavior are very different, as you'll see. Aggressiveness is characterized by a disregard for the rights of others. Aggressive statements put others down, and humiliate or embarrass them. They often show contempt. They are embedded in a "if-I-win-you-lose" mentality.

You can easily see those elements in the manager's aggressive statement. The employee has been goofing off. He has repaid the manager's trust and generosity by taking advantage of the manager. He plays games with the manager. Well, the manager insists that's all going to stop!

What are the likely consequences of the aggressive approach? Probably a short-term flurry of activity by the subordinate to get the job done, although how well it will be done is questionable. The priority at the moment is, overwhelmingly, to finish quickly.

The long-term results could be self-defeating for the manager. The subordinate's resentment over having been put down will probably never entirely dissipate. The manager will not get the future commitments he might wish from this subordinate. He may even lose the subordinate, who is indeed guilty of delay, although not necessarily of plotting it.

Many people who make aggressive statements don't mean to be offensive. Often it's a matter of not really knowing how to deal with negative feelings or how to express themselves. Sometimes, not knowing how to express their wants and emotions, they suppress feelings such as anger or anxiety. Later, something will trigger an emotional outburst, and they lose control of what they say. It's a page from conventional wisdom: If you don't control your temper, it will control you. Aggressiveness often results from feelings having been suppressed until they erupt.

Because aggressiveness usually creates negative feelings in the subordinate, it is not appropriate managerial behavior. Aggressiveness may *not* end an unpleasant situation, it may even promote its continuation.

Aggressiveness and nonassertiveness, as the chart at the bottom of this page shows, are two extremes in the behavior of communicating.

Assertiveness is a moderate form of behavior that seeks to change a situation or a behavior in another. The assertive statement expresses your feelings and protects your rights, without disregarding how the other person feels or sees his or her rights. It asserts your dignity without trampling on the other person's. Assertiveness involves being open and forthright as well as respectful. In contrast, aggressiveness usually involves being manipulative, underhanded, and contemptuous. To be aggressive is to be destructive; to be assertive is to be constructive.

For example, suppose the manager

Aggressiveness	Assertiveness	Nonassertiveness
Totally you, excluding others	Primarily you, secondarily others	Totally others, excluding you

in the opening example of nonassertiveness and the later one of aggressiveness had chosen to make an assertive statement. Here's how it might go:

"It seems to me that the job I assigned you should have been completed by now. I don't know at what stage you are because you haven't given a progress report. I have to tell you that I'm disturbed by both facts —that you aren't finished and you aren't keeping me up to date. I want that to change. Starting now, I want progress reports, and I also want assurances that you will avoid further delays. If the job isn't completed in a reasonable time, I have to tell you that I shall take that fact into account in considering you for future responsibility."

That typical assertive statement consisted of four elements or steps:

1. **A description of what is going on.** The manager expected the job to be finished by now, but it isn't.
2. **An expression of how the manager feels about what is going on.** The manager is disturbed by the fact that the job isn't finished and that there are no progress reports. He doesn't know at what stage the job is.
3. **His definition of the change that he'd like to see take place.** The manager wants progress reports and reassurances that the work will be completed in a reasonable time.
4. **A clear statement of the benefits to the other person in making the change.** This manager lets the subordinate know that how he finishes this job will influence the manager's thinking in making future assignments or in giving the subordinate further responsibility. In short, produce as I

think you ought to, or this may be as far as you go.

The important benefit to the manager in the preceding illustration is that he has taken control of a situation that he had permitted to happen. Assertive people do take control. Nonassertive people give up that control. Assertive people stand up for themselves. Nonassertive people abdicate their rights. In terms of Transactional Analysis, their words, manner of speaking, and body language say, "You are okay, but I am not okay."

In the assertive statement, you can almost see the manager's posture and hear his voice. Assertive people maintain eye contact. Their gestures are natural and proportionate to what they say. Their tempo is moderate, not slow and halting or aggressively fast. The tone and volume fit the words. If they are angry, the pitch goes up, and so does the volume.

They stand or sit firmly. They don't slouch. In psychological terms, they are "congruent." Words, posture, and gestures are all an integral part of the message. When you hear an assertive person, you do not receive mixed messages, gestures, or body language that conveys one message while the words convey another.

Benefits of Assertiveness

The assertive approach accomplishes several clear and positive objectives for you.

One benefit is that you confront issues, not personalities. The issues are clearly drawn. For example, in the previous illustration, the job was not finished. In confronting the issues squarely, you avoid getting trapped into discussing personalities. The subordinate may indeed be inefficient or deceitful. He may be playing games. But to judge his character or his motives is to risk blurring the issues that you have to resolve. The resultant discussion (or, more likely, argument) may wander along many paths, none leading to the solution you seek. Therefore, define the issues and stick with them. Let others know exactly what is on your mind.

If the other person tries to sidetrack the discussion by suggesting that you are being unreasonable, or that there are all sorts of barriers to getting the job done, you simply stick with the issues: "The job is taking a long time and I'm not being kept informed. I want that changed."

A second benefit to you of assertive behavior is that you release your feelings. It's healthy to express your feelings, especially when they are negative. Strong emotions that are suppressed don't go away. They eventually seek an outlet, and that outlet may be aggressive behavior. Getting your feelings out will relieve the tension, possibly in both of you. The employee, who knows that things are not right between you, will appreciate your having cleared the air.

A third benefit of assertiveness has been touched on, but deserves elaboration. As manager, you need to have the feeling that you are in control, not a victim of circumstances that you cannot control. Your being assertive enables you to take control. Then you can guide the interaction toward your objective: the change of behavior you want in the other person. Control, in the context of assertiveness, is different from domination. When you control, you guide the transaction toward your objective; you do not push or force.

You have a better chance of getting what you want when you make your objective known. You may not always get what you want entirely, but by stating your objective, you can talk about the issues. The other person knows where you stand. There is room for discussion and negotiation.

Consistent assertive behavior brings you more than the immediate objectives of confronting issues, getting your feelings out, and controlling the discussion. It establishes you as a credible and trustworthy person. You acquire a reputation as a person who is straightforward; a person who says, "This is what I see. This is what I want." People come to feel that they know where they stand with you.

Assertiveness increases your influence with others. They know that in a transaction with you they can get right to negotiating with you, discussing what is happening and what may have to be done about it. They don't have to expend valuable time and energy wondering if you are being completely honest with them.

When people realize that they see the real you, they tend to listen more intently, to grant you more of their attention. And if you get people to listen carefully to what you have to say, you are well on the way to exerting a stronger influence over them.

Finally, your assertiveness encourages people to want to work with and for you. They don't have to wonder what your position is on an issue. They don't have to worry about your attacking them personally, since you have acquired a reputation for sticking to the issues. They don't have to try to interpret your real feelings, since you reveal them yourself.

All in all, you are a person others can believe and trust. Being assertive doesn't necessarily make you liked among your employees. After all, you tell them what they may not want to hear. But they don't have to like you. They **do** have to respect you. And they will.

An Action Plan Calling for Assertiveness

1. Description of the problem that exists between you and _____

_____ (employee's name): _____

_____

_____

_____

_____

_____

_____

_____

_____

2. An explanation of your decision to be assertive in dealing with the problem:

_____

_____

_____

_____

_____

_____

3. Previous interviews with the employee during which the problem was discussed and action agreed upon:

Date: _____ Action: _____

_____

_____

_____

_____

Date: _____ Action: _____

_____

_____

_____

_____

_____

Date: _____ Action: _____

_____

_____

_____

_____

4. How you intend to resolve the problem assertively.
   A. A description of what is going on: _____

_____

_____

_____

_____

_____

_____

_____

_____

_____

_____

B. How you feel about what is going on: _____

_____

_____

_____

_____

_____

C. The change you want to see take place: _____

_____

_____

_____

_____

_____

_____

_____

_____

_____

D. The benefits to the employee of making the change: _____

_____

_____

_____

_____

_____

_____

_____

5. Date of interview: _____ Was the change described in 4C agreed upon?   Yes ☐   No ☐
If not, describe the change that is to take place: _____

_____

_____

_____

_____

_____

_____

_____

Time frame for change: _____
Proposed action if change does not take place within the time specified:

_____

_____

_____

_____

One of your primary objectives in adopting assertive behavior is to get more of what you want more often. But you can't hope to get what you want from others without their cooperation. You can increase your chances of success by more closely involving the other person. You want the other person to be more responsive to you. And you must be more responsive to him or her.

Responsiveness

As admirable as the assertive mode is, used exclusively it would create vast deficiencies in communicating. Every transaction involves at least two sets of needs and wants, at least two people asserting what is important and valuable to each. If neither listens and responds to the other, there will be a stalemate. Think about all those unproductive meetings you've attended where it appeared that people seemed not to hear anyone but themselves. What is needed, therefore, is a responsive mode of behavior as well as an assertive mode. A scale that reflects this appears at the bottom of this page.

The four elements of responsiveness are:

1. Seeks information. In assertiveness, you describe what is going on. In responsiveness, you seek to find out how the other person sees the situation.

2. Asks about the other's feelings (or accepts the feelings of the other without necessarily agreeing with them). Just as you believe it is important to get your feelings out, so that the other person knows where you are, it is helpful to find out how the other person feels. This is especially valuable in conflict situations because it frequently reveals that the other person is upset by the conflict, just as you are. Once the feelings are expressed, you should accept that the other person does indeed feel the way he or she describes. You don't have to agree that the feelings are justified; you just have to accept that the other person has them.

3. Seeks change of behavior in self. You may find that your perception of and reaction to a situation are neither helpful nor appropriate. In that case, you might find a way to change your behavior to be more fitting or to get the results you want.

4. Sells self on the benefits of change. Chances are you won't make a change of behavior unless it is valuable for you to do so. Find the reward.

Depending on the results they want, most people choose between assertiveness and responsiveness. When you decide to listen, when you want information from another that you think could be useful, you are responsive. For example, a subordinate falls behind on her work. She misses deadlines. You're upset about it, because you've always been impressed with her conscientiousness. You call her into the office for a talk.

You: I want to talk with you about your work. You're missing deadlines, something you never did before. I'm worried about the way your performance has fallen off.
Subordinate: I'm worried, too, but I'm more than worried. I'm angry.
You: Why are you angry?

You started by being assertive. But the subordinate is giving you some information you believe you must have in order to really understand what's behind the missed deadlines. So, you adopt a responsive mode of behavior.

Subordinate: Because you're really piling on the work these days. I know we've cut back on people, and that I have to work harder with less help. But I can't remember when I've had to juggle so many schedules and

Aggressiveness	Assertiveness	Responsiveness	Nonassertiveness
Totally you, excluding others	Primarily you, secondarily others	Primarily others, secondarily you	Totally others, excluding you

jobs as I do now. You're really loading me up.

You: Can you be more specific?

Subordinate: Sure, I can. You give me complicated jobs to do, then before I've had a chance to complete them, you change the due date on me. Sometimes you interrupt me in the middle of one job with a rush job to do. First thing I know, I have two tight deadlines. I never have the satisfaction of getting on top of the job.

You: So you're saying that I'm creating a lot of the problem?

Subordinate: Yes. I need to have a schedule I can depend on. Also I need to be able to finish one project before having to do another, unless there's an out-and-out emergency.

You: Okay. From now on, I'll keep a written schedule of what I've assigned you. That way, I'll know what you're working on and when it's due. And when I see you're jammed up, I'll find someone else to give the work to.

You've defined a change of behavior in yourself. The benefits are clear. You're not only going to get better work out of a valued subordinate, but you will have an employee who feels better about working for you.

You might choose a responsive mode from the outset. Some of the occasions when you might find it advantageous to be responsive rather than assertive are when you . . .

. . . take over a new operation and want to learn about the environment, culture, constraints.

. . . are counseling people who have a performance problem. You have to draw them out to find out how they view the problem or to get an agreement that a problem exists.

. . . are in a situation that calls for sympathy, patience, and understanding, such as an employee's loss or tragedy.

. . . are listening to someone you respect and admire.

. . . are confronted by a person in an intense emotional state, when it is clearly not to your advantage to counter assertion or aggression with your own assertion.

. . . are in a group situation when it is desirable to encourage others to take leadership.

. . . are receiving feedback from employees as to conditions in the department or characteristics of your leadership.

Responsiveness as a frequent approach in dealing with employees may put you in a subordinate position or make you appear passive or reactive. Use the responsive mode judiciously.

Assertiveness	Responsiveness
Gives information	Seeks information
Expresses feelings	Seeks to know and accepts the feelings of the other without necessarily agreeing with them
Describes behavior change desired in the other	Seeks a change of behavior in self
"Sells" benefits of the change to the other	"Sells" self on the benefits of making the change

An Action Plan Calling for Responsiveness

1. How the issue is to be resolved responsively:
   A. The employee's description of what is going on: _____

   _____

   _____

   _____

   _____

   _____

   _____

   B. How the employee feels about what is going on: _____

   _____

   _____

   _____

   _____

   _____

   _____

   C. What changes you might make to improve the situation, resolve a problem, to incorporate a suggestion, etc.: _____

   _____

   _____

   _____

   _____

———————————————————————————

———————————————————————————

———————————————————————————

———————————————————————————

D. The benefits to you of making such a change: _____

———————————————————————————

———————————————————————————

———————————————————————————

———————————————————————————

———————————————————————————

———————————————————————————

———————————————————————————

2. Date of interview: _____
   Time frame for change:

———————————————————————————

Date for next discussion, if any:

———————————————————————————

Assertiveness-Responsiveness

Some transactions or discussions between manager and employee are a mixture of assertive and responsive. In assertive-responsive behavior, you exchange information and feelings. You seek a change in behavior jointly, with benefits for both of you. The approach has several specific characteristics: It . . .

. . . acknowledges the rights and feelings of each person in a transaction.

. . . creates a dialogue situation in which each person feels comfortable expressing feelings about what is going on.

. . . recognizes that each person has wants, needs, and resources. The resolution or outcome need not be all one person's effort.

The following chart shows how the modes of behavior look on the scale reproduced previously:

The assertive-responsive approach is especially useful in problem-solving, coaching, counseling, and conflict situations. The description on the preceding scale is realistic: In any normal, healthy interaction with others, you are unlikely to give up your primacy entirely. No matter how strongly you wish to be responsive as well as assertive, there will be at least a slight predominance of your assertiveness.

To illustrate the flexibility that a good manager of people must have, the following is an interview that takes place between a manager, Blake, and a key supervisor, Geraldine, whose nickname is Gerry. The occasion is a quarterly performance evaluation of Gerry. Blake has been reviewing the goals that the two had agreed on the previous quarter.

Blake: You've done a good job reaching your goals with one exception.
Gerry: I know. The self-directed work team isn't functioning.
Blake: Right. We agreed last quarter that you would set up the work team that would function semiautonomously. You didn't feel, as I recall, there would be any big difficulty about having the team working by now. And we can't even think about extending the idea to the whole operation until we see how this group works. Has there been any progress?
Gerry: It's not really a team, not yet. I've talked to the various members, and they're pretty excited, but that's it.
Blake: Want to bring me up to date?

How would you describe Blake's mode of behavior up to this point? Is it assertive, responsive, or assertive-responsive?

_____

_____

Blake is describing what he sees as going on, or rather, what should be going on, as opposed to what is reality. Then he seeks information from Gerry about how she sees it. When both people are giving information, the predominant mode would be **assertive-responsive.**

Gerry: My plan was to organize the team around Mac Wright. But, as you know, he got caught up in the maintenance training program. That was full-time. He's just now getting off it and I've been coaching him.
Blake: Did you know from the start that he'd be tied up for this long?
Gerry: No one seemed to know how long it was going to take to

Aggressiveness	Assertiveness	Assertiveness-Responsiveness	Responsiveness	Nonassertiveness
Totally you, excluding others	Primarily you, secondarily others	Almost equally you and others	Primarily others, secondarily you	Totally others, excluding you

get that program set up. But after a couple of weeks, I figured I was going to have to wait.

Blake: Wasn't there anyone else in the department who might have been able to fill in for Mac?

Gerry: As I think back, maybe Phil Jordan. But at the time, Mac was almost perfect, and I didn't want a possible second best.

Blake: So you never had a fall-back plan.

Gerry: No.

How would you describe Blake's behavior in the last segment?

_____

_____

Blake is gathering information. He is, therefore, more in the **responsive** mode than anything else.

Blake: I have to criticize you for not having a contingency plan.

Gerry: Well, as I said, Mac was coming back. I thought, sooner rather than later. He was excited about helping me for this new team. If I had replaced him, it would have been a big blow to him. Besides, he was by far the best person.

Blake: I understand, but we didn't make the schedule, which I think was important to do.

Gerry: Frankly, I thought having the best person was more important than a tentative schedule.

Blake: I don't agree that the project should have been held up. We set an objective: that you would have a self-directed team working experimentally by the end of the quarter. You decided to change our schedule without consulting me. For the future, I want you to assure me that when

we set an objective, you won't change it unilaterally.

How would you describe Blake's behavior here?

_____

_____

Taking the data he has received from Gerry, Blake describes the situation as he perceives it and tells Gerry how he feels about what he sees. Blake is being **assertive,** of course.

Gerry: Okay, Blake, I'm sorry. But to be fair to me, you haven't been altogether accessible. First, you were sick, then for a time, while you got better, you worked half days. Then you had to fill in for the boss while he was on vacation. You let it be known around the department that you would appreciate our taking care of any problems we could. I made some decisions on my own, and I guess I made some wrong ones.

Blake: I won't question the other decisions you made, but do you really believe the postponement was right to do on your own? On such an important project?

Gerry: I guess not.

Blake: There may be times in the future when I'll get tied up. But when it comes to an important objective, I'll never be too tied up to see you. I'll make time. I'm sure I would have this last time if I'd known what you were doing.

Gerry: I hear you.

How would you describe the mode(s) of behavior in this last segment? _____

_____

The modes of behavior are first, **responsiveness,** then **assertiveness,** and finally, the promise of **responsiveness** in the future.

> *Blake:* Now that that is settled, let's talk about the forthcoming quarter. I'm anxious to get the experimental unit under way. Are you still excited about it?
> *Gerry:* Mac's available and raring to go. So am I.
> *Blake:* Great. What do we need to do to get it launched?

By expressing what he wants, and by soliciting Gerry's ideas, Blake has returned to an **assertive-responsive** mode. Interestingly, Blake moved from appraisal to counseling to criticism back to goal-setting, varying his behaviors to match the needs of the particular phase he was in.

As you can see, while assertiveness is essential to the success of a manager, it is also important to involve your subordinates in decisions, plans, and actions that affect them. That's why assertiveness, responsiveness, and some combination of the two are all necessary and important behaviors in your repertory.

An Action Plan Calling for Assertiveness-Responsiveness

1. Description of a problem or a need for discussion with _____

_____ (employee's name): _____

_____

_____

_____

_____

_____

_____

_____

_____

2. Previous interviews with the employee concerning the issue, with conclusions or actions agreed upon:

Date: _____ Action or conclusion: _____

_____

_____

_____

_____

Date: _____ Action or conclusion: _____

_____

_____

_____

_____

3. How you intend to resolve the problem or issue assertively-responsively:
   A. Your description of what is going on: _____

_____

_____

_____

_____

_____

_____

A(1). Your description of what the other person believes is going on: _____

_____

_____

_____

_____

_____

_____

A(2). How the other person describes what is going on (in the discussion): _

_____

_____

_____

_____

_____

_____

_____

B. How you feel about what is going on: _____

_____

_____

_____

_____

_____

B(1). How you believe the other person feels about what is going on: _____

_____

_____

_____

_____

_____

B(2). How the other person actually feels about what is going on (in the discussion): _____

_____

_____

_____

_____

_____

_____

C. What change would you make that might help to resolve the problem or issue? _____

_____

_____

_____

_____

_____

_____

_____

C(1). What change could the other person make that might help to resolve the problem or issue? _____

_____

_____

_____

_____

C(2). Describe the actual changes in you and/or the other person that have been agreed upon in the discussion: _____

_____

_____

_____

_____

_____

_____

_____

_____

_____

_____

_____

_____

D. The benefits to you of making the proposed change: _____

_____

_____

_____

_____

_____

_____

D(1). The benefits to the other person from making the proposed change: _

_____

_____

_____

_____

_____

_____

_____

_____

_____

_____

4. Date of interview: _____

Time frame for change: _____

Date for next discussion, if any: _____

Your Assertiveness Profile

	Yes	No
1. Other people do not regularly initiate discussions with you.	_____	_____
2. Your statements to others often seem to arouse defensive responses.	_____	_____
3. In many of your business and personal relationships, you suspect that you give much more than you receive.	_____	_____
4. People seem excessively tactful or diplomatic in giving you disappointing news.	_____	_____
5. You sometimes suspect that people try to dominate you.	_____	_____
6. When you attempt to be humorous, people laugh hesitantly or without conviction.	_____	_____
7. You suspect that other people are reluctant to bring problems to you.	_____	_____
8. You believe there is something impolite about saying, "I want you to . . ."	_____	_____

9. People often respond to your questions or opinions with brief answers.

_____   _____

10. Frequently you have the feeling that you are not in the mainstream, e.g., socially, organizationally, politically, etc.

_____   _____

11. You are convinced that you have the right to make your wishes, needs, beliefs known to the people you work with.

_____   _____

12. When you have a conflict or disagreement with people you work with, you find, generally, that they are willing to join with you in a search for a solution.

_____   _____

13. In a meeting, other attendees do not address you directly—or they do so rarely.

_____   _____

14. Other people tend to offer unsolicited advice to you on the way you do things.

_____   _____

15. Often, in your dealings with others, you suspect they are just being polite.

_____   _____

16. People often seem nervous or otherwise uncomfortable around you.

_____   _____

17. People usually avoid eye contact with you.

_____   _____

18. You have many acquaintances but wonder whether you lack a satisfying number of substantial relationships.

_____   _____

19. You like to be in control and frequently move to establish your control or leadership.

_____   _____

20. When you are distressed or angry, you usually express how you feel.

_____   _____

21. People are guarded in their conversations with you, causing you to wonder whether they are telling you what is really on their minds.

_____   _____

22. You often suspect that people don't bring you information about what is happening in your department.

_____   _____

23. When you do not like the conditions under which you are working, you take steps to change them or to persuade others to change them.

_____   _____

24. When in conflict with others, your tendency is to deal with the issues of the conflict rather than the personalities of the disputants.

_____   _____

25. Your ideas often aren't taken seriously by people you work with.

_____   _____

26. You usually deal with unpleasantness with humor.

_____   _____

27. In disagreement or in tense situations with others, you often feel frustrated because you cannot express how you feel. _____ _____

28. You frequently sense that people don't really listen to you. _____ _____

29. You are used to hearing the criticism that you are not firm enough in dealing with others, that you are "too easy." _____ _____

30. You regard yourself as an expert on your feelings and perceptions, and you tend to regard others as experts on theirs. _____ _____

31. You are accustomed to having people tell and show you that they trust and believe you. _____ _____

32. When you have a problem to work out with another, you allow ample time for the other person to express his or her feelings and encourage that person to do so, even when that other person seems hostile to you. _____ _____

Yes to the following questions indicates behavior tendencies toward:

Aggressiveness	Assertiveness	Responsiveness
1	11	3
2	12	4
6	19	5
7	20	8
9	23	10
13	24	14
16	30	15
17	31	18
21	32	25
22		26
		27
		28
		29

Using Influence and Persuasion

Unquestionably, the manager of today's work force depends much more on influencing and persuading than on coercing. Contemporary employees want to be taken seriously, persuaded, negotiated with. The manager who knows how to deal with subordinates in these ways usually achieves greater produc-tivity, loyalty, and cooperation than managers who practice a more authoritarian style of management. Successful managers sell, rather than tell.

Some managers are better at it than others. Following are some of the characteristics of people who have better-than-average persuasive powers:

1. They know what they want.

This is no small thing. Persuaders have goals, and they are careful not to lose sight of those goals. They *own* their wants. They want to win, although they are realistic enough to know that they cannot win at the expense of others if they are to build long-term relationships.

They know they have a right to try to get what they want. You are manager. You have responsibilities and goals. You have every right to ask that employees join with you in the realization of your goals.

3. They are articulate. Not only do persuasive people know what they want, they know how to express those wants. They may not use the words "I want," but they know how to translate their wants and needs into terms that others can accept.

4. They are sensitive. Successful persuaders are sensitive to what others might want from and contribute to the transaction. They are skillful at sensing the verbal and nonverbal language of others. More importantly, they strive to include others; they know that the other person must be involved. They also know that in a transaction the other person, in this case an employee, has something to contribute—knowledge, experience, ideas, needs and resources, all of which can be helpful.

Experienced persuaders are also sensitive to time and situation. There is a time and place for everything, and they are ever alert to how, when, and where to go for certain kinds of actions.

5. They have credibility. Influential people have a reputation for dealing squarely without abandoning their own interests. They are careful not to run roughshod over others. They know that to influence others, they must be respected and trusted. Credibility is probably the single most important characteristic of the successful persuader. Real believability takes a long time to build, but not very long to destroy.

Credibility has to do with others' trust in you. People listening to you must be confident that you will not knowingly deceive them. Making a mistake in fact or judgment is one thing. People you work with can forgive you for that. But if you are guilty of deception, you may find your credibility shattered beyond repair.

Employees trust that while you are pursuing your own interests, you are looking after theirs as well.

6. They know how to deal with opposition. People who are skilled at persuading others anticipate opposition and know how to handle it. It's very important when you're dealing with employees not to be automatically threatened and defensive when they don't always and immediately agree with you. Persuasive managers even welcome a certain amount of open opposition, because hidden opposition is difficult to deal with. Also, objections openly expressed can be tested and verified. If the objections are real, then the persuader has learned something, and knows what must be done to achieve the objective. Obviously, handling opposition effectively depends upon getting the other person involved in the transaction. Their responses to objections are geared to keeping the door to communication and persuasion open.

7. They know how to ask for the "order." Persuaders know that people have an urge to complete a task or a transaction. They know how to get action from employees, to persuade the employees to agree to a contract with the managers.

8. They know what motivates others. Good persuaders understand that what motivates people to act is (1) the value that people believe they'll gain as the result of an action; and (2) the accessibility or attainability of that reward. It not only has to be valuable to them, but their chances of getting it must be real. The successful persuader uncovers the value and makes it possible for the other person to have and enjoy it.

In summary, when persuasive people have an idea, proposal project, or task, they:

- **Make it interesting**—Otherwise what is being said won't be listened to;
- **Make it valuable**—It must appeal to the self-interests of others; and
- **Make it easy**—If it isn't seen as do-able, then it won't be done.

Five Rules of Persuasion

Managers don't often think of themselves in sales transactions with employees, but that's everyday reality. They sell their goals and standards, their methods, their feedback, their relationships. They sell when they assign responsibility and tasks, when they seek results and productivity. Telling employees to do this or that doesn't, as any experienced manager knows, automatically get you what you want. Employees, if they choose, can delay, do a barely acceptable job, sometimes get out of doing it entirely. Employees know how to frustrate and subvert.

Managing these days is influencing. How well you influence depends, as has been stated, on your credibility, on the respect people have for you. It also depends on your persuasive skills. To be completely successful, you must apply the following five rules of persuasion:

1. Know your product. It may be an idea, a project, loyalty to you, your goals, the well-being of the de-

partment. Whatever you are selling, know what you have to offer. You cannot reasonably hope to persuade anyone of anything until you have first been able to convince them that you know what you are talking about. In your selling, employees expect you to be congruent: what you present is the real you. What you say you want, is what you really want. There is no deception, no manipulation.

2. Know your prospect. Your prospects, as a manager, are your employees. You have to know something of their needs and wants. It isn't enough to sell your needs and wants. You must translate them into benefits that meet the others' needs. When you are dealing with an employee, you ask yourself questions such as the following:

- What parts of your proposition would interest him or her?
- How can you best describe those benefits?
- What kind of words would you use?
- Is this a good time for the employee to hear what you have to say?
- Would he or she be more receptive on another occasion, in another place? What tone of voice do you use?
- How detailed should you be?
- Should your approach be formal or informal, friendly or professional?

The answers to such questions can be found, in part, in your knowledge of the other person.

Persuasion does not occur on a strictly rational level. Your listener will respond to your presentation in a number of ways—rationally, emotionally, intuitively—and it is essential to anticipate some of these responses. Employees have biases, psychological sets, and preconceptions that you must be sensitive to. For example, if you are a highly educated manager speaking to employees of limited education and vocabulary, you would pick and choose your words with care, lest you be misunderstood, not understood at all, or resented.

3. Involve your prospect. In a transaction, communications do not flow one way. Certainly, in your encounters with employees, you don't want such a restricted flow. The other person brings ideas, biases, strengths, wants, and needs to the transaction, and you need to hear whether they might affect your getting what you want. Besides, you need to get feedback on how well you are doing in your persuading. So take the prospect's temperature from time to time. Ask questions such as, "Am I making myself clear?" or, "Does this make sense?" or "Do you see what I'm getting at?"

Another reason why you need to get the other person involved is that many people have trouble listening. They are not trained to listen well. They tend to hear only part of what you say, or what they wish to hear—which may be a quite different message from the one you intend to give. Through your questions and invitations to respond, you can find out what they have heard.

Even people who listen well have limited attention spans. If you don't change pace, if you don't get their participation, their minds wander. They stop hearing.

4. Ask for action. Don't hesitate to let the other person know what you want to happen as a result of the dialogue. You may want an idea from the other, acceptance of your ideas or standards, agreement to take on a responsibility, adoption of your methodology, commitment to your goals,

etc. Make sure you spell it out. Don't assume that the other person always knows what you are selling or what you expect of him or her.

Managers often are frustrated because they leave an employee with what they believe are clear instructions for action, but discover later that the action never took place. The clarity and the purpose were mostly in the manager's mind.

5. Be prepared to handle opposition. Opposition to new ideas is natural to many people. Employees don't feel the need to jump just because the manager wants it. When you introduce change—in procedures and methods, in behavior, etc.—you can expect resistance. You should expect it. Few people listen attentively, surmount their biases easily, or surrender to someone else's ideas or wishes, even if that someone is the boss.

Unfortunately, many managers tend to take opposition personally. They believe that the resistance is directed against them as managers, not against the ideas or the changes. The fact is that opposition usually indicates the need for more persuading. A positive way to look at opposition, the way salespeople look at it, is to recognize that the person who fights you is involved. Nothing is worse than the employee who hears you out, then ignores you.

Being persuasive is knowing the techniques, what makes them work, and how to apply them. The techniques themselves are rather simple. But "thinking them" and then applying them are more complicated. "Thinking them" means being aware of them, having the intention to use them, and to use them skillfully. It helps for you to think of yourself as an influencer. Most managers tend to think of themselves as *the boss*, and that can get in the way of a selling image.

How Is Your Communicating Know-How?

	Yes	No	Not Sure
1. How you communicate with your employees is as important as what you say.	_____	_____	_____
2. Aggressiveness is the mark of a good leader.	_____	_____	_____
3. Aggressive statements are characterized by putting people down, embarrassing or humiliating them.	_____	_____	_____
4. A frequent reason why people make aggressive statements to others is that they don't know how to deal with their negative feelings or how to express them.	_____	_____	_____
5. Aggressiveness may result in short-term change, but long-term damage.	_____	_____	_____
6. Employees tend to shun making contacts with an aggressive manager.	_____	_____	_____
7. It's acceptable for a manager to be nonassertive when he or she isn't sure what decision to make.	_____	_____	_____
8. Usually the reason why the nonassertive manager does not achieve objectives or maintain standards is because no one is sure what they are.	_____	_____	_____
9. An assertive statement conveys what you want without stepping on the other person.	_____	_____	_____
10. An assertive statement has four elements: your perception of what is going on; how you feel about it; the change you want the other person to make; and why that person should make it.	_____	_____	_____
11. Assertiveness is the most desirable approach in managerial communicating with employees.	_____	_____	_____
12. A truly assertive statement helps you to confront an issue rather than another person.	_____	_____	_____
13. Consistent assertive behavior helps to establish you as a credible and trustworthy person.	_____	_____	_____

14. One drawback to assertiveness is that it controls behavior.   _____ _____ _____

15. You are usually liked more by others when you are assertive.   _____ _____ _____

16. In a transaction between two people, success is achieved only if one person is assertive and the other is responsive.   _____ _____ _____

17. Responsiveness is normally not a recommended way for a manager to behave when communicating with employees.   _____ _____ _____

18. Responsiveness involves agreeing with the feelings of the other person.   _____ _____ _____

19. Responsiveness is often appropriate when you are in the initial phase of taking over an operation that is new to you.   _____ _____ _____

20. When counseling an employee on a work-related problem, you may find that being responsive encourages the employee to give you information that you might not have learned otherwise.   _____ _____ _____

21. Responsiveness is appropriate in any interaction in which you suspect that the other person brings knowledge or resources to the discussion that could be useful in solving a problem or a conflict.   _____ _____ _____

22. When you are responsive to employees, you involve them, an important factor in their motivation.   _____ _____ _____

23. If your predominant mode of behavior is responsive, you may find other people getting what they want from you without your achieving your interests.   _____ _____ _____

24. Predominantly responsive people sometimes find that their ideas are not seriously taken by others.   _____ _____ _____

25. You will usually find that you should be more assertive than responsive when counseling an employee on a performance problem on which no corrective action has been taken.   _____ _____ _____

26. Aggressiveness and nonassertiveness are never appropriate behaviors in managing people.

_____ _____ _____

27. Not being assertive is probably one of the most common reasons for managerial failure.

_____ _____ _____

28. Most successful managers alternate between assertive and responsive behavior, even in the same interview.

_____ _____ _____

29. Being assertive is often an effective way to approach conflict that exists between you and your boss or another manager.

_____ _____ _____

30. The assertive-responsive mode helps ensure that you stick to issues in a conflict rather than personalities.

_____ _____ _____

The following is a memo written by an executive who is concerned about objectionable activities and behavior on the part of his employees. Analyze its tone. How would you characterize it?

To all employees:

It has come to my attention that a number of our work policies are being violated, extensively. Since these policies have been in force for many years and have been disseminated widely and periodically, it is difficult for me to believe that those who are violating them are without knowledge of the facts. Therefore, I must conclude that the violations are willful, and I must warn you that further willful violations will not be tolerated.

The policies that are most frequently being ignored are the following:

a. Start work times. All employees are expected to be at their work stations promptly at 8:00 in the morning, not at 8:10 or 8:15.

b. Breaks. There are two breaks per day, one in the morning, and the other in the afternoon. Each break lasts ten minutes, not fifteen, not twenty minutes. When the bell rings signaling the end of the break, you are expected to commence work **without delay.**

c. End of day. Work continues until 5:00. That does not mean 4:45 Or 4:50. Washup for plant employees is permitted at 4:45.

I realize that many of you are loyal and conscientious workers. It seems a shame that a group of laggards reflects poorly on others. Supervisors are expected to enforce these policies without exception.

Write your analysis of the memo and its effect here:

_____

_____

_____

_____

_____

_____

Author's analysis of the memo:
The tone of the memo is aggressive.
The writer assumes that exceptions
to the rules or policies are willful,
people want to break them. The
"violators" are also characterized as
laggards.

While the complaint of this executive may be justified, and while the
writer does give information on what
is happening, the memo is more sarcastic than businesslike. The memo
impugns the integrity of some of the
employees; it's a put-down. Therefore, it must be characterized as aggressive.

The sarcastic, humiliating tone
will probably have an adverse effect
on everyone, violators and nonvio-
lators. The latter will probably still
feel threatened because the harsh
tone could be turned against them,
in the future, for some reason. The
memo will not, in all likelihood, have
the impact the writer wishes.

What changes would you make in
it to make it less aggressive, yet still
assertive? Write your version below:

_____

_____

_____

_____

_____

_____

_____

_____

_____

_____

_____

_____

_____

_____

_____

See the following suggested rewrite, with which you can compare yours.

To all employees:

Through the years, your company has invested substantial time, money, and other resources to develop a set of policies that we believe are fair to the company and to employees. These policies have been in force for a number of years and have contributed greatly to the success of our operation.

In order to continue to ensure that success, and to provide a standard working environment for everyone, the company requires strict adherence to the policies. Accordingly:

1. Starting time. Everyone is expected to be at his or her work station by 8:00 A.M. Any alterations to this routine will inconvenience all.

2. Breaks. Two breaks are allowed each day, one in the morning and one in the after-noon. Each lasts a maximum of ten minutes. Stretching the breaks throws everyone's schedule off. The bell lets you know when time is up.

3. End of work day. Quitting time for our facility is 5:00 P.M. The **only** variation occurs in the plant, where employees may begin their washup at 4:45.

We appreciate all your efforts to follow these policies. They also apply to supervisors, who are charged with seeing that they are complied with. Because over-looking violations would not be fair to the employees who observe them faithfully, we caution that disciplinary measures will be applied to those who do not observe them.

Thank you for your cooperation in this matter.

Following are a number of statements. Analyze them to determine whether they are aggressive, assertive, assertive-responsive, responsive, or nonassertive.

1. One of your salesmen, Peter, seems to you to be falling down on the job. For the past three weeks, his call reports show that he has not made the required number of new business calls that you have established.

You: How's your golf game these days, Peter?
Peter: About what it's always been. I haven't had much time to play lately.
You: That's surprising. I figured you must be working on getting your handicap down these days.
Peter: Why?
You: Well, you're certainly not making sales calls.

Is your mode of behavior . . .

aggressive _____
assertive _____
responsive _____
assertive-responsive _____
nonassertive _____

2. You have been concerned about the declining performance of one of your key people, Janine. You have always believed that you could depend on Janine to take on almost any assignment with enthusiasm and skill. Recently, another key member of your staff became seriously ill and had to be out of the office for several weeks more. You asked Janine to assume some of the ill person's responsibilities. At first, she was cooperative and willing to work long hours. But then a perceptible decline in both the quality and quantity of her work began to occur. You schedule a discussion with Janine.

You: I'm worried about the fact that your work is suffering. That's really not like you. For example, I asked for an interim report on the Artsie project three days ago, and I haven't heard a word about it. I don't think I've ever known you to miss a deadline.
Janine: And I've never known when I had so much work to do. Not only do I have all of my responsibilities, but you've added Jeremy's as well. I'm flattered, but I'm exhausted, too. I think you have to assume some blame for this. It seems to me that every time we get jammed up here with work, I'm the one you think of to help break the jam. It's a sort of discrimination. I think I'd feel better if you discriminated against someone else in the department for a change.

You: I'm a bit surprised to hear this. If you feel that I've discriminated against you, I can understand that you would be upset, and possibly demotivated. I'd like to hear your suggestions on how I might better distribute the work. You and I both know, Janine, that others on the staff have certain limitations. But if you can come up with some practical suggestions that will alleviate your burden, I'll consider them and make what changes I can. After all, you are quite valuable to me. I want to make it possible for you to operate at peak effectiveness and feel good about what you do.

Is your mode of behavior . . .

aggressive _____
assertive _____
responsive _____
assertive-responsive _____
nonassertive _____

3. A few weeks ago, you appointed a task force to work on the utilization of PCs in your department. By this time you hoped to have some recommendations, if not a system designed. But you haven't, and you're not sure why. You call the chairperson of the task force to your office.

You: How's the task force coming along? I haven't heard anything, so I'm wondering what's happening.
Chairman: We've run into a string of bad luck. Barney couldn't free himself for a few days, so we had to wait for him. First, we spent some time gathering some data, but it wasn't correct. We had to go back for

more. Then, we've had two people out sick. But we should be ready to go now.

You: I hope so. I guess there's not much you can do when people get sick. But maybe now . . .

Is your mode of behavior . . .

aggressive _____
assertive _____
responsive _____
assertive-responsive _____
nonassertive _____

4. From time to time one of your employees has sought advice from you regarding his financial situation, which, to be blunt, has bordered on bankruptcy. He is in your office again today, asking for suggestions. As you think about previous discussions, you realize that while your troubled subordinate has listened to you—or seemed to—you doubt that he has ever taken your counsel. Consequently, you believe, he has continued to make some serious mistakes.

You: I don't understand why you come to me asking for my advice, Burt. I've given it to you frequently in the past year, and I honestly can't see that you've followed any of my suggestions. I don't like saying this, but if you don't intend to take my advice, then I wish you wouldn't take up my time asking for it.

Is your mode of behavior . . .

aggressive _____
assertive _____
responsive _____
assertive-responsive _____
nonassertive _____

5. One of your more talented and bright employees can be erratic in her work behavior. She seems to delight in taking on responsibilities, but she tends to resist taking suggestions from you on how she might best do the work assigned. You have tried, tactfully, to persuade her to adopt some of your methods in getting the work done, but without results. Her response has been uniformly, "I am more comfortable with my own techniques, and I think they work just as well." Unfortunately, they haven't. They have resulted in poor scheduling, rushing just before deadlines, and error. You see the same consequences developing on the latest project you have assigned her, and to head off further complications, you decide to discuss the situation with her.

You: Amy, on past jobs I have made some suggestions about methods and approaches you might follow. Generally, you've tended to stick with your own. And I was willing to have you do so as long as they worked equally well. But I'm convinced that your methods do not work as well. Let me tell you what I've seen. I've seen a lack of planning, and that results in last-minute tying up of loose ends. In the last two projects, we've had to take an extra day or two so you could comb out the mistakes that I think would not have been there if you had progressed in a more methodical manner. In the manner I prescribed. I'm unhappy about the errors. I'm unhappy about the frantic last-minute activity, because we have to reschedule a lot of other work to give you the time you need on the project. Now the same patterns are developing on the current project. I want you to set down on paper, before you go any further with the project itself, a schedule that you can follow that will avoid that last-minute pressure. And lessen the chance for errors to creep in. I have to insist that you follow my suggestions. If you don't, I will have to think seriously about asking you to take on a similar project in the future.

Is your mode of behavior . . .

aggressive _____
assertive _____
responsive _____
assertive-responsive _____
nonassertive _____

6. You are distressed to receive an angry phone call from one of your company's largest and most profitable customers. He tells you that he received an erroneous invoice for a recent, sizable shipment and that he called one of your subordinates about the error. The subordinate treated him discourteously, which made him consider the possibility of switching his business. You call the subordinate to your office and criticize him.

You: Mr. Robins called me to tell me of the bad treatment he received from you. I guess you don't realize that Mr. Robins is one of our most valuable cus-

tomers, and he and others pay our salaries. Therefore, it's shocking for me to hear that you could be rude and patronizing to such a man on the telephone when he calls about an error that we've made. Get this and get it straight. If I ever again hear that you've been anything but courteous and eager to service a customer, if I ever get the idea that you are smart-aleck on the phone, I'll come down to your department and replace you so fast you won't know what happened until you pick yourself up off the street. I can't tolerate people who don't have brains enough to know how to treat a good customer.

Is your mode of behavior . . .

aggressive _____
assertive _____
responsive _____
assertive-responsive _____
nonassertive _____

7. You are a division-level executive and you are meeting with your general manager, branch operations, for a six-months performance evaluation. The blank lines in the left margin are for the second part of the exercise, about which you will receive instructions later. The first part of the exercise is to determine your mode of behavior.

1. _____

2. _____

You: Alan, you and I agreed six months ago that you would add six branch offices by this date. And that all six would be fully staffed. Is that your understanding of what we agreed to in the previous evaluation session?
Alan: That's right.

3. _____

4. _____

5. _____

6. _____

7. _____

8. _____

9. _____

10. _____

11. _____
12. _____

13. _____

14. _____

You: However, during these past six months, the increase has been only four, and one of these four has only a branch manager and an assistant. Correct?

Alan: You're correct.

You: I have to say that I'm quite disappointed at these results. At our previous meeting, my memory is that you didn't think the goal of six was unrealistic. In fact, I think you were the one who suggested the number six. So I would gather you're not very happy with your results either.

Alan: I'm not happy. I don't think, however, that it is entirely my fault that we didn't make the goals.

You: I've worked with you a long time, Alan. So when you say you're not happy, I believe that. Still, the goals are important. And there's the matter of your having fallen short the previous six months. Those goals were only 85 percent met. The question is, what has to happen for us to reach these goals?

Alan: I think the weakness in my operation is that I've been trying to handle the administrative tasks here as well as operate in the field. I'm training my assistant to take over more of the inside work. That will free me to spend about one-third more time in the field.

You: Okay. Let's set the same goals for the next six months. But it will be absolutely necessary that the goals be met—100 percent. Is that all right with you?

Alan: Fine

You: Here's what we'll do. Instead of waiting six months to evaluate your performance, we'll meet every two months to measure progress toward the goals. I'll provide whatever resources I can. If, however, you can't make it this time, then I think you should know I'll probably ask you for your resignation. If you do make it, it will be reflected in your evaluation, of course.

Is your mode of behavior . . .

aggressive _____

assertive _____

responsive _____

assertive-responsive _____

nonassertive _____

At this point, go back to situation number seven. In the left margin are lines at points where some aspect of assertiveness-responsiveness is expressed.

Fill out each line with one of the following aspects.

Assertiveness	Responsiveness
Giving information	Seeking information
Expressing feelings	Asking about feelings (or accepting feelings)
Defining change	Defining change in self
Giving benefits of change	Giving benefits of change

Answers to

Communicating Know-how

1. Yes
2. No
3. Yes
4. Yes
5. Yes
6. Yes
7. No
8. Yes
9. Yes
10. Yes
11. No. Depending on the situation, the desirable approach may be assertive, responsive, or assertive-responsive.
12. Yes
13. Yes
14. No. Controlling an interaction means that you guide it to a desired conclusion. You do not force or manipulate it. Controlling can be positive behavior, as opposed to dominating, which often has negative consequences.
15. Not sure. Assertiveness engenders trust and respect, not necessarily feelings of affection.
16. Not sure. This may be true in some transactions, but often both people assume both modes of behavior at various times.
17. No. It is legitimate behavior in certain transactions.
18. No. It means accepting, without necessarily agreeing.
19. Yes
20. Yes
21. Yes
22. Yes
23. Yes
24. Yes
25. Yes
26. Yes
27. Yes
28. Yes
29. Yes
30. Yes

Answers to the Seven Situations

1. Aggressive. Being sarcastic and assuming the salesperson is not making calls because he is playing golf is a put-down.
2. Responsive. You seek information and offer to change yourself.
3. Nonassertive
4. Assertive
5. Assertive
6. Aggressive. The tone and words used are humiliating.
7. Assertive-responsive

Answers to Second Exercise

1. Giving information
2. Seeking information
3. Giving information
4. Seeking information
5. Expressing feelings
6. Asking about feelings
7. Accepting feelings
8. Giving information
9. Seeking information
10. Giving information
11. Defining change
12. Seeking information
13. Defining change in self
14. Benefits of change

Chapter Three

Enhancing the Motivation of Your Subordinates

If you are like most managers, you are benefiting from only a portion of the motivational power that is available to you in your subordinates. In participative management, you work to help your employees enter into a partnership with you. As you have read, most of your employees want to do a good job, for themselves as well as for you. Work is very important to them, satisfying many of their growth, self-esteem, achievement and social needs. How effective your employees are in accomplishing mutual objectives depends, in large part, on how well you manage their motivation. That's quite different from motivating them, a phrase many managers use. In fact, you cannot motivate anyone but yourself. But you can enhance the motivating forces within your subordinates. You can help them to do a better job for you.

Underlying this section on motivation are the following truths about the behavior of people at work. They are managerial facts of life.

1. People have reasons for what they do. They have objectives, and they choose among them. Behavior, as the psychologist would say, does not occur in a vacuum. It is directional. Managers complain that their employees are not motivated. This is plainly not true. Whether or not the manager understands why people behave as they do, be assured that the employees do have reasons. They have chosen to behave as they do.

2. Whatever people choose to do, they do it to gain something they believe is good for them. Not only is the behavior directed toward a goal, that goal must be valuable to the doer. People often choose between courses of action, all of which may represent some value. They'll choose the one that seems to promise the most value, the biggest reward, all other things being equal. The reward may be internal, that is, the doer wants to achieve something, gain satisfaction, indulge himself or herself. Or the value of choosing a particular way of behaving may lie in external rewards: It may lead to money, or a promotion, or some other reward that comes from others.

When people choose a course of action and gain the reward they seek, they are psychologically reinforced. That's an important fact for the manager. Behavior that is reinforced is likely to be repeated. If a subordinate does a good job, and you reward/reinforce that subordinate, he or she will tend to repeat the effective behavior.

3. Whatever reward or goal a person chooses must be attainable. People do not choose a course of action *solely* because it is valuable to them. They have to believe they have a reasonable chance to gain the reward. Most people won't make the effort to go after a reward, no matter how valuable it may be, if the chances of getting it are slim. There may be many employees who would like to be president of the company, but for most of them, the presidency will be a fantasy, not a goal. Getting there is too "iffy."

4. The situation surrounding the work can affect its value to the employee or the employee's expectations of success in doing it. The conditions under which a job is done mean much to employees. For example, Sarah would like to be a branch manager, but she doesn't

want to accept a branch 2000 miles away. Ted may want a transfer, but not if it means working for a particular vice president whom he dislikes. Francine wants more money, but the job that will give it to her means that she will have to leave her friends to work in another office across town. Philip wants more responsibility, but the job he'll move into will require working overtime on nights and on weekends, and he dislikes the thought of being away from his family.

5. You, the manager, can increase the value of the work, can help raise the employee's expectations of being rewarded for the work, and can enhance the situation surrounding the performance. This is the most important thing for you to know. It gives you tremendous influence over the productivity of the people who report to you. You have at your disposal many ways to increase the value of the work by providing rewards for good performance. You can call on any number of resources that help the employee to do a better job and to build his or her confidence.

In short, you can play a major role in the motivation of your subordinates to work harder and better. If you are a successful manager, you'll achieve your goals; you'll recognize that a large part of that success is due to the commitment and performance of your employees. In turn, you are the key to that commitment and performance. A manager can leave subordinates to work disappointingly, or help them to perform outstandingly.

Your Motivation Quotient

	Agree	Disagree	Not Sure
1. People who are motivated to work usually perform better on the job.	_____	_____	_____
2. Correcting poor work attitudes in employees is an important part of the manager's job.	_____	_____	_____
3. If people had a choice of working or not working, most people would choose not to work.	_____	_____	_____
4. Some people are unmotivated, and there is nothing the manager can do with them.	_____	_____	_____
5. In general, people won't work at something they don't like to do.	_____	_____	_____
6. Motivation is an important key to effective performance.	_____	_____	_____
7. The attitudes that a manager has about subordinates can affect the work they do.	_____	_____	_____
8. Low employee morale is one of the biggest obstacles to good performance in a work group.	_____	_____	_____
9. Most people work primarily for money.	_____	_____	_____
10. Fear is an effective way to motivate people.	_____	_____	_____
11. Motivating employees is a manager's most important responsibility.	_____	_____	_____
12. The style of managing plays an important role in employee motivation.	_____	_____	_____
13. Managers who are nice to their employees get better performance.	_____	_____	_____
14. Few people welcome criticism of their work.	_____	_____	_____
15. People today seem to want to know what's in it for them before taking a job.	_____	_____	_____
16. Working conditions can affect the degree of motivation in employees.	_____	_____	_____

	Agree	Disagree	Not Sure
17. People always want to be rewarded for doing what they're supposed to do.	_____	_____	_____
18. The truth is that most people have to be coerced and controlled by the manager to put forth adequate work.	_____	_____	_____
19. The average employee will not be committed to a task or a job that he or she doesn't find valuable.	_____	_____	_____
20. Whether people in a work group are strongly motivated or not depends largely on the way they are managed.	_____	_____	_____
21. When employees suspect that they will have difficulty doing a certain kind of work, they will usually lose motivation to do that work.	_____	_____	_____
22. A manager can often make work more desirable to an employee.	_____	_____	_____
23. Employees will choose not to do any kind of work that is not valuable.	_____	_____	_____
24. Most employees value job security above almost anything else.	_____	_____	_____
25. Managers have the ability to increase the value of work in employees' eyes as well as their confidence in their ability to do it.	_____	_____	_____

Making the Job More Valuable

You can increase the value of the work by making sure that employees feel rewarded for doing it. While money and promotions are obvious rewards, you may be surprised at the variety of other reinforcers you have available. Some of them are internal; some, external.

Internal reinforcers are generated within the person. Employees give themselves their own rewards. They have their personal goals that consti-tute value to them. For example, there are employees who work to be able to afford material goods or a certain life-style. The work itself may be of secondary interest, but that does not necessarily mean that they don't perform it well. Quite the contrary. Such a person is interested in doing it well enough to earn raises and to achieve job security. However, since this person looks for challenge and fulfillment away from the job, he or she may be reluctant to take on complicated new responsibilities or substantial risks that may threaten his or her situation. You would be ill-advised to push such a person in a new direction without minimizing the possibilities or consequences of failure.

Some people work to satisfy their need to belong, what psychologists call social or affiliation needs. They work well and conscientiously in groups, less efficiently in tasks that require them to work apart from others. (For example, people with strong affiliation needs often make poor salespeople.)

Esteem, their own as well as others', is something important for some people on the job. Actually, the two are often linked. As the others' esteem for them increases, it reinforces their self-esteem. Esteem-seekers are moderately competitive. They want more than to be accepted by others. They want respect, and that often involves winning over others. Therefore, the esteem-seeker will usually seek achievement and responsibility. But remember that the competitive spirit is moderate. This person likes to win, but probably not at the expense of alienating others.

There are people who move toward power. They tend to be political and to take risks where they believe there is a reasonable chance for payoff. These people may commit themselves to do whatever is required to gain responsibility and influence over others. So long as they work for you, they will probably be among your key subordinates. But to retain them, you will have to provide greater and greater responsibility and influence opportunities.

There is a power-seeker of a different kind who will usually prove to be a continuing asset to you: the employee who seeks personal power of freedom. Having power means having options or choices. Having freedom means much the same thing. This employee wants freedom over work, the opportunity to choose the kind of work done and the means to do it. If you can delegate and let these employees off the leash, you'll find they are a joy.

Mixed in with all these other motivations is the need to achieve. It leads to self-esteem, power, freedom, a sense of growth and self-satisfaction. The true achiever needs change, challenge, and moderate risk.

Most of the internal reinforcers you'll recognize will fall among these five: a sense of growth and progress on the job, status, achievement, self-esteem, and social needs. You'll go with the grain if you can assign work that permits employees to achieve their personal goals. The work becomes valuable, automatically, to them. When you call attention to what it can help them accomplish, you are giving the employee something to look forward to. See the exercise that follows for various ways to help employees recognize the internal rewards that await successful completion of the work.

Here is a list of internal reinforcers/rewards that are motivating factors in employees:

a. **A sense of growth.** People can derive satisfaction out of knowing something new or having a skill this year that they did not have last year. Remember Herzberg's satisfier/motivator *advancement:* an actual improvement in status or position.

b. **Status.** Where is the employee now in the organization and in the department? What kind of prestige is enjoyed? How can the status be increased?

c. **Achievement.** What milestones has the person reached? What accomplishments is he or she proud of?

d. Self-esteem. How much value or worth does the person feel?

e. Social needs. It is important for people to be accepted by the group. It is possible for you to suggest ways, through accomplishment or change of behavior, to increase that acceptance.

Test your understanding of internal reinforcers/rewards by matching the numbers of the proper reinforcer to the statements listed below. Use the letters a, b, c, d, or e.

Reinforcer/Reward

1. "The way you're expanding your knowledge of our classifications and procedures, you'll be the best-informed person in this department." _____

2. "Having a chance to coach the new person will give you a sense of how much progress you've made." _____

3. "I've heard from your colleagues that you're a good person to consult when there's a problem." _____

4. "I've never known anyone to grasp our systems as fast as you have." _____

5. "If you suspect that you are one of the most valuable people we've had in this department, you're correct." _____

6. "Other people in the department tell me they really appreciate the unselfish way you jump in and give people a hand when there's a pile-up." _____

7. "The course in quantitative decision-making that you're taking at night will make you a more decisive supervisor." _____

8. "No one else, since I've been department head, has ever increased productivity so quickly after being hired." _____

9. "I can tell you that it's consensus that your reports are not only the most thorough, but the most concise we've ever seen." _____

10. "Doesn't it give you a feeling of satisfaction to know that your section has the lowest absenteeism rate in the division?" _____

As a manager, you shouldn't assume that employees automatically have a sense of achievement or satisfaction when they make progress or fulfill an objective. Ironically, they may not recognize their achievement. You are in a position to guide their thinking on what has to be done, and to help them recognize when they have done it well.

You can discover what is important to an employee through observation, performance records, and by interviewing; although in the latter case, you and the employee will have to have built a base of trust. Employees will have to feel that they can rely on you to take them seriously and to respect their interests.

If you worry about invading an employee's privacy, use the form on page 88. The top half is for employees to spell out, in private, those objectives that the employee would like to accomplish through the work —money, advancement, education, more skills, etc. Then in the second half of the form, the part you see, the employee translates those personal objectives into job-related tasks and assignments that will help him or her achieve those objectives.

Your performance appraisals should also give you a clue as to what kind of work the employee prefers and does well. In addition to your existing records, you can supplement your knowledge by filling out, or having the employee fill out, the Employee Preference Questionnaire. (See page 117.)

All of the data you gather can be used to maintain an up-to-date Employee Personal Data Form, (see page 119) that can guide you in making assignments, planning training, preparing for periodic coaching for growth and development, etc. Both of the above-mentioned forms are to be found in this section.

Your knowledge of people's preferences, needs, and goals can help you in assigning them to tasks and jobs in which they will feel more satisfied and will probably perform more effectively. You want them to value what they are doing so that they will see the advantages to themselves in doing the work well.

External Rewards

Usually the most desirable and potent reward is an internal reinforcer backed up by one that is external. External rewards are those that you, the manager, confer on employees in recognition of their good performance.

As mentioned, raises and promotions are common examples of external rewards. But there are many other ways to recognize and reinforce an employee's performance.

Take some time and fill in as many of the following blanks as you can with any kind of a reward that is in your power to give. To help you generate some ideas, think of ways in which your managers rewarded you. Rewards can be tangible or intangible (for example, a memo circulated to the department describing one employee's achievement).

_____

_____

_____

_____

_____

_____

_____

_____

_____

_____

———————————————————————

———————————————————————

———————————————————————

———————————————————————

There are many kinds of external rewards. Three that are usually readily available are: (1) more work; (2) training; and (3) more of you.

1. More work. Herzberg regards the work itself as a motivator. If it is successfully done, then more work might be a reinforcer. You can't just pile on more work. It should be interesting and challenging work. The assignment should be accompanied by the message, "Because you have handled your responsibilities so successfully, I'm going to let you have even more responsibility." If you pull down the responsibility from a level higher than the employee's, you are, in Herzberg's terms, enriching the person's job. It's called *vertical loading.* You are loading the employee's job with responsibilities higher than he or she would normally enjoy. You'll find some suggestions for loading in the section on Delegation (page 96). A task force can be a stretching experience for your good performers (see page 207).

Not everyone will be motivated to undertake more responsibility. But changes are good that there are people reporting to you who are not getting all they want and can handle.

You can provide more satisfying work for your superior subordinates by finding out what they like to do best and by providing more opportunities for them to do it. (See the preceding section on internal rewards.)

2. Training. Surprisingly little recognition is given to the fact that most people want to grow on the job.

They don't want to have the feeling that they are stuck, that they continue to do the same thing year after year. Training and education can help people to develop their potential. Training, however, is often presented as a way to correct a deficiency. And indeed it is. But if this is the context in which training is presented, then most people will tend to think of it in negative terms.

Make training and education rewards for successful performance. They are given in recognition of the fact that employees want to increase knowledge and skills. Make it known that the people who have first crack at any learning opportunity are the people who perform well.

Most training and education are seen as work-related. But don't rule out courses, seminars, workshops, and lectures that broaden the perspective and deepen the thinking of the participants, even if those learning opportunities don't relate directly to everyday effectiveness on the job. And the more personal the benefit from the training, the greater the probability that the experience will be seen as a reward for good performance.

3. More of you. You can be a reward. For example, your esteem for a subordinate could be very important to that person. If you assign a job that you regard as special, let your subordinate know that your esteem of his or her ability is what led you to make the assignment.

Consider that an employee will view freer access to you as a recognition of that person's value to you. Managers have a way of letting it be known that, even though their schedules are crowded, they can usually find time for certain valued people. That access doesn't have to be strictly formal or one-way. You might make it a practice to drop by subordinates' offices, desks, or work stations for a short chat. Those informal occasions with better-performing subordinates constitute a clear message to them and to others.

One way to increase access and express esteem is by consulting with key people. You say to such a subordinate, "I'd like to get your opinion on something." It may be a project that is planned or in the initial stages, a potential new employee, a restructuring of the department or procedures, etc. You don't have to adopt all of the suggestions, but you must be sincere in seeking them out.

Do you occasionally sit down with a subordinate who performs well and offer coaching and career counseling? Most people in organizations don't get the help they need in planning their careers. You occupy a vantage point. You know more than your subordinates about what is happening or is about to happen in the organization, the opportunities that are opening up, the career paths that have proved to be the most promising.

Finally, there is your concern. You are interested in helping the employee to become even more valuable to the organization. You can express your concern on a personal level. "You've been working awfully hard lately. Why don't you leave early Friday?"

The above are three major categories of external rewards. Some others are:

• **More desirable workplace.** Yes, of course, a corner office. But it doesn't have to be so elaborate—a new desk or chair, a rug, a divider or a door on the office, or a more preferred location.

• **Recognition.** People who accomplish in a superior manner usually like the fact to be known—by memo, a notice on the bulletin board, a letter to your manager about them, perhaps an article in the organization's paper.

• **More freedom.** A subordinate is given the chance to set some of his working hours. The chance to do office work at home is prized by some. People may select their own methods. You may free them from having their work checked by others and rely on them for accuracy.

Providing more freedom for an employee is a reinforcer too seldom utilized by managers. That's surprising, especially in view of the fact that many key performers have demonstrated their ability to work without close supervision. Making it official is a message that will be understood and appreciated. The privileges don't have to be extensive. They do, however, have to be seen not as lax management or indifference, but as a reward for deserving service.

• **Equipment.** A more expensive typewriter, a two-line phone, a personal terminal, or PC. Ask yourself, "What kind of equipment will make this person's job easier?"

• **Opportunity to represent you.** Give a valuable employee a chance to chair a meeting for you or to represent you at a meeting you can't attend. If a client comes calling, let the employee take him or her to lunch.

Check with the list on page 75 for more ideas on external rewards.

Some managers seem to have an inordinate fear of favoritism that prevents them from doling out rewards on an individual basis. But as a manager, you should accord special treatment to those employees who perform well and willingly to achieve your objectives. If you are careful to extend special consideration to those employees who do a good job, and to limit such consideration to that group of performers, you will then clearly convey the message, "This is what I do for people who work according to my standards. Do a good job, and you will enjoy similar benefits." That kind of favoritism clearly works in your favor.

Increasing the Chances for Success

No matter how attractive a goal is, no matter how desirable a reward is, most people are not likely to try for it unless they see a reasonable chance that they will reach it. Their perceptions, their expectations of success are what matter. As a manager, you may feel at times that you have to be a psychic to judge how employees see their ability to do a job or an assignment. You hope that they'll tell you how they feel about their chances of being successful at a task or a responsibility. Sometimes they don't.

In making assignments, or at the first sign of performance problems in a job, you should be careful not to assume that a subordinate will volunteer that he or she is worried about being able to do the job.

The best time to deal with an employee's low expectation of success is before the work is undertaken. If you suspect that an employee is floundering in a job, or is less than enthusiastic about finishing an assignment, consider asking questions that will uncover the employee's hesitancy or concern. For example, do you foresee—or are you running into—any problems doing this work? What, in your opinion, is the best way to go about this task? Is there anything I, or anyone else, can do to help you do a more successful job? Do you feel there are obstacles to your doing a better job that we might be able to eliminate?

There are steps you should almost always take in assigning a task or a job that will help increase the employee's expectation of achieving success:

1. Define the task as precisely as possible. One of the most common managerial failings is taking for granted that the other person knows what the manager wants. And one of the most common reasons that people see difficulties in performance is that they're not sure about what is to be done.

Think in terms of output. What do you want to happen as a result of the employee's activity? Talk as specifically as possible about what you expect to be done, about the output.

2. Set standards. Tell *how* the job is to be done, now that you've defined what will happen as a result of the methodology. What are the minimally acceptable standards? You want 250 phone calls per week, but under no circumstances will you accept less than 200. The minimum, however, won't earn any medals.

Standards include a time frame—so much activity within a certain period of time. On tasks that will take a long time, it's a good idea to estimate that time period. You may think in terms of six months, while the employee worries that you want it in six weeks. Furthermore, indicate how rigid or flexible the time frame is. Knowing that the schedule can be negotiated may ease any problems an employee foresees in doing the work.

3. Describe the resources available. Telling subordinates what help is available to them can go far to allay doubts or fears about doing the work. For example:

Authority. If you're going to define responsibility, it's only fair to tell the employee how much authority he or she will have to do the job. How many people will be reporting to the subordinate? For how long? Will the reporting be full- or part-time? What decisions can be made by the subordinate? Does the subordinate have the power to hire, fire, transfer, or discipline? What can the employee do without having to check with you?

People. Where are the people to come from? If the subordinate will be sharing employees with another manager, you may have to lend a hand in the negotiating process with that manager.

Equipment. What office or production equipment will be needed? How should the employee go about getting it? Will access to a computer be helpful? Perhaps you can't make a complete inventory of equipment in advance, but your assurances that reasonable equipment needs will be met can contribute much to an employee's confidence in successful performance.

Facilities. Where can the work be done? Will the conference room be available for meetings? Should the office layout be rearranged to provide groupings of employees? Is there spare office space available?

Experts. You may wish to refer subordinates to advisors or consultants in personnel, training, marketing, and/or research both from inside and outside the organization. What are the budgetary limitations? There may be other employees or managers who are experienced in the kind of work you want done, and you can steer your subordinate to them for consultation and guidance. Or you may be that expert resource.

Precedents and guidelines. Others' experience in similar jobs or tasks can be an encouraging launching pad. Your own experience can help you develop guidelines and suggestions. Naturally, you don't want to spell everything out so completely that there's no challenge, no room for the subordinate to bring his or her talents to bear on the job. But you do want to make sure that the subordinate knows all of the resources, including and especially you, that are available.

When you detect an employee's reservation about the chances of successfully performing an assignment, or when you see signs of demotivation due to fear of failure, you may want to take one or more of the following steps to bolster self-confidence:

1. Relief from other duties. Sometimes the employee doesn't consider the individual assignment too difficult, but the total work load looks formidable. State your priorities, and be prepared to lighten the load if necessary.

2. Offer to collaborate. You upgrade yourself from a resource to an active partner. There may be times when your experience, skills, and knowledge are needed, or would really push the project along. It would be a good idea to imply that the employee would still get the greater sense of achievement and glory if you became a partner.

3. Provide protection. You take care of any interference from others that might hamper your subordinate. Protecting employees from distracting events and people is one of the most important functions of a manager. It is especially vital during a special assignment that takes the employee somewhat out of the usual, predictable duties.

4. Remove organizational barriers. In most organizations, horizontal communications are weak. Employees often find communicating and cooperating across functional lines of authority difficult, primarily because the authority is different. Rather than having the employee ask for permission to deal with a co-worker in another line of authority, set up a special arrangement with the other department head so that your subordinate can operate without asking for permission each time.

5. Provide training. This is the most obvious step to take when an employee seems hesitant about his or her ability to do the job. Training doesn't have to be formal. You might be able to arrange for some coaching sessions with someone who has the expertise that the employee needs. Sitting with a more experienced person can be useful.

6. Coach. Some timely coaching may be needed, especially when an employee feels overwhelmed by a sense of inadequacy or incompetence. Many people have these feelings when they confront a task that is different from or more complicated than what they've been accustomed to, or when they've had a failure or two. That's time for you to schedule a session in which you can review those talents and past successes that have led to your selecting him or her. You may have to lead the employee through the assignment step by step.

7. Break the job down into smaller units. Perhaps the task as a whole looks more formidable than it needs to. Find a way of defining the job in stages. The subordinate might indicate at which stage help would be required—and what kind. Breaking the task into steps, parts, or stages can help the subordinate build confidence and a sense of achievement as each step is completed.

8. Expand the timetable. If an employee feels the pressure of a deadline, and if it's possible, let him or her know that the schedule is somewhat flexible. You may have to play an active and continuing role in assuring that deadlines are met. It is helpful to have intermediate goals so you can check on progress. Some employees seem unable to gauge the time required. Discreet monitoring by you is in order.

No discussion of a time allocation is complete without realizing that an employee may need a deadline to do the job. For many people, open-ended schedules result in procrastination. You may have to negotiate a deadline acceptable to both of you. Once you agree on the deadline, unless some significant variable occurs that the two of you had not anticipated, insist that the deadline be honored.

Your important job is to help the subordinate develop a higher expectation of achievement in an assignment or continuing function. The toughest job you have is not coming up with answers, but knowing what to apply to whom and when; when to take a more active or passive role; when to monitor the work overtly— or discreetly.

Creating the Right Conditions

There are, in general, four kinds of conditions that can affect the value of work to the employee or the employee's expectation of achievement or success in doing the work: the work climate or environment, physical environment, geographical location, and personal factors.

Work climate. Most people prefer to work in a climate that is friendly and collaborative, with people supporting one another rather than fighting or undermining them. You should intervene when excessive conflict between subordinates gets in the way of results. You can reduce tension and anxious feelings in subordinates by making efforts to be more predictable, to apply similar standards to everyone, to reward the results you want, and to discourage behavior that is unreasonable, political, competitive, and divisive.

Bear in mind that when you assign an employee to an atmosphere that is tense, combative, ferociously competitive, and constrictive, you'll very likely see a reduction in the person's motivation.

Physical environment. The physical conditions that surround people as they work can affect their perception of the value of the work or their ability to do it well. Production managers will tell you that people tend to work better it a plant or facility that is kept orderly and neat, in which housekeeping is strictly enforced. A person who likes a great deal of social contact on the job will not be eager to accept an assignment sitting alone in a room or in a corner with a computer terminal, no matter how much pay is involved. An employee who tends to be claustrophobic will probably feel unable to perform in a small, closed-in space. A person who has been used to privacy might find working in a large, open area very distracting. You may see a demotivating effect when you assign a salesperson to an inner-city territory that is run-down, dirty, and in the person's mind, dangerous.

There is always the possibility that the employee will relate the physical environment to status. It's safe to say that most people would prefer a physical environment that is clean, secure, attractive, and comfortable. Transferring an employee from a surrounding that is less so to one that is more congenial may increase the value of the work.

Geographical location. Some people don't want to live in a large metropolitan area such as New York City. Others don't want to feel stuck in a small town in the Midwest, South, or Far West. People who are athletic, who like the outdoors, who ski, would probably go for an assignment in New England. Some people would like to work in the Sunbelt. A salesperson might object to a large territory if he or she doesn't like travel.

Personal factors. It may be difficult for you to determine that personal factors inhibit an employee's enthusiasm for an assignment. A pending divorce, an illness in the family, a wish to devote more time to spouse and children, all can figure in when an employee is evaluating a responsibility or a transfer.

You need to know, yet how much can you ask? How much do you really want to know? Where regular performance has been slipping, you may need assurance that the reasons are more personal than job-related. At least with that knowledge, you can recommend outside counseling.

Sometimes you can't do anything about the situation. Someone must work for an unpleasant boss, or take an assignment in the inner city, or work in an unpleasant office or plant environment. In such cases, look for ways to increase the value. Perhaps you can increase the person's compensation, add a title, a promise of first crack at the next promotion, etc. Or give the employee some sense of control in a bad situation by asking how the job could be changed to make it more attractive. You may be able to make some alterations that you hadn't thought of. Your concern can often go a long way toward compensating for the adverse conditions under which the employee has to work.

What can you do when you cannot increase the value of the work or make it a bit easier? Here are some options:

● **Assign a time limit.** Perhaps you can offer a time limit of a few months or a year at the outside. When people know that there will be an end to less-than-ideal conditions, their tolerance often goes up.

● **Extra support.** Offer more access to you. Be more attentive and understanding when employees call upon you.

● **Make a special plea.** Put it on the basis of the employee's doing a favor to you by accepting adverse conditions. Express your appreciation. Making an occasional personal plea or request for a favor is quite in line.

While it's true that the situation can detract from its motivational value, it's also true that situational factors may enhance motivation. You may have to look harder, but the chance is that someone will respond favorably to what others would regard as adverse circumstances.

Basically there are five steps that can enhance the motivating forces in your subordinates:

1. **Tell them what you expect them to do.** Include them in your goal-setting (see Setting Goals and Measuring Performance). Convey your standards and your expectations that employees will do a good job. Your positive expectations will often affect their performance positively. You are more likely to get the results you want if you express expectations that you will get them.

2. **Make the job valuable.** Review the rewards at your disposal. Assign tasks on the basis of employee preference if possible. Recognize the internal rewards in your employees and activate their recognition of those rewards.

3. **Make the job do-able.** Review the steps outlined earlier in this section for helping the employee to believe he or she can do a good job.

4. **Give them feedback.** While they're trying to do what you want them to do, tell them how they're doing—well, or not so well. They need to know, so that they can make corrections or continue to do what they're doing right.

5. **Reward them.** When they've done what you expected them to do, recognize their efforts.

Reward on a consistent, regular basis.

A Checklist of Rewards

1. Adding to the present responsibilities tasks and duties from the same level (job enlargement)
2. Adding responsibility from a higher level (job enrichment)
3. Rotating the employee among jobs to increase skills and provide variety
4. Assignment to a committee or task force
5. Freer and quicker access to you
6. Establishing an informal relationship with the subordinate
7. Seeking the employee's opinions and suggestions
8. Advising the employee on career and organizational opportunities
9. Providing information on the organization that is not confidential, but not well-known
10. Showing your concern for the employee's well-being
11. Revealing something of yourself by talking about your problems or experiences
12. Training
13. Coaching
14. Spending more than average time on appraisal
15. Promising more money
16. Praising
17. Promising a promotion or more responsibility
18. A more desirable office, work space, or better furniture
19. New or better equipment
20. Giving more freedom to select their assignments
21. Giving more freedom to set their work hours
22. Chance to do office work at home occasionally
23. Providing opportunities to work without close supervision or monitoring
24. Chairing a meeting for you
25. Representing you at an interdepartmental or higher-level meeting
26. A business trip
27. Taking a client to lunch, dinner, or to an entertainment event
28. A chance to accompany you to a meeting, on a trip, etc.
29. Preference in selecting vacations or overtime
30. A day or half day off
31. Lunch or dinner on the organization
32. Encouragement to do outside work with a professional or volunteer organization
33. A party
34. A gift—plant, book, something for the desk, etc.
35. Filling in for you when you're away
36. Preferred assignments
37. "Thank you"

A Demotivation Diagnosticator

Are there signs of demotivation in your department? How strong or serious are they? Following is a list of symptoms of demotivation that you can check against what you see in your own operation. As you reflect on each symptom, consider whether it appears frequently, sometimes or occasionally, or rarely or not at all.

	Frequently	Sometimes	Rarely
1. People gossip cynically about the organization.	_____	_____	_____

2. There are widespread petty grievances and complaints.   _____   _____   _____

3. Employees make sarcastic comments about the organization and its management.   _____   _____   _____

4. People seem hesitant to submit suggestions for better operation in your department.   _____   _____   _____

5. You hear comments such as "All you can do is hang in" or "The name of the game is survival."   _____   _____   _____

6. There is a pronounced "Them vs. Us" when employees talk about higher management.   _____   _____   _____

7. Covert conversations take place among employees from which you are conspicuously excluded.   _____   _____   _____

8. You hear employees say, "What's the point in killing yourself?"   _____   _____   _____

9. Absenteeism is high and occurs also among employees who once had exemplary work attendance records.   _____   _____   _____

10. While employees carry out your instructions, they are noticeably reluctant to offer to take on responsibility.   _____   _____   _____

11. People who have demonstrated a high ability to work well now seem to turn in assignments that are minimally acceptable in quality or quantity.   _____   _____   _____

12. Employees label management policies and decisions as unfair.   _____   _____   _____

13. Employees procrastinate and miss deadlines.   _____   _____   _____

14. People seem bored and fatigued.   _____   _____   _____

15. Your departmental employees seem to develop strong cliques.   _____   _____   _____

16. Employees who used to be ambitious now seem cynical about their chances to get ahead on merit within the organization.   _____   _____   _____

17. Employees whom you always viewed as reliable now openly display resentment when asked to take on extra work.   _____   _____   _____

18. Employees seem to give up quickly and seek help from you when engaged in a demanding or complex task. _____ _____ _____

19. Organizational rules are scorned and ignored. _____ _____ _____

20. Lateness has increased among your employees. _____ _____ _____

21. Employees spend organizational time doing personal tasks or making personal telephone calls. _____ _____ _____

22. There are frequent unexplained absences from offices, desks, or work stations. _____ _____ _____

23. There is disproportionate complaining about wages and salaries. _____ _____ _____

24. Employees grumble about working conditions. _____ _____ _____

25. Employees do not take proper care of equipment. _____ _____ _____

26. Employees are reluctant to stay after hours even to finish work that could be completed in a short time. _____ _____ _____

27. People do not seem to listen carefully when you give instructions. _____ _____ _____

28. Your subordinates spend inordinate time doing relatively simple tasks. _____ _____ _____

29. Your hear employees make references to how well off their friends and acquaintances are in other organizations. _____ _____ _____

30. Employees complain loudly that too many objectives come down from higher management for them to meet. _____ _____ _____

31. There are complaints from employees that higher management sets conflicting priorities that make it difficult for them to work effectively. _____ _____ _____

32. You have to follow up your assignments of tasks and responsibilities to make sure they are done correctly and on time. _____ _____ _____

33. Employees seem unwilling to pitch in and help co-workers. _____ _____ _____

34. There is a neglect of routine chores.

35. Employees rationalize sloppy and erroneous work.

36. You hear frequent complaints from employees about what they consider errors on the part of top management.

37. Subordinates make belittling comments about the capability of higher management.

38. In meetings with representatives of higher management, employees sit silently, but then become active in after-the-meeting discussions among themselves.

39. Employees complain bitterly about what they regard as preferential treatment given to others whose performance is not outstanding.

40. Some subordinates complain that other employees are not carrying their share of the work load.

41. You sense that one or more employees have become informal leaders in the department, in covert opposition to your authority.

42. When you make rounds of your department, you are struck by the widespread socializing you see.

43. There are complaints from employees that management is out to manipulate or take advantage of them.

44. There are mistakes and incompleteness even in routine work that employees have always performed well.

45. Employees seem reluctant to discuss their long-range plans with you.

46. There is inordinate resistance to and grumbling about even minor changes in policy or procedures.

47. Employees appear to need monitoring by you in order to apply themselves to their work.   _____   _____   _____

48. You feel a need to give pep talks to employees to energize them to do the work.   _____   _____   _____

49. There are unpredictable delays and snafus.   _____   _____   _____

50. Employees who formerly seemed easygoing and relaxed now display tension and irritability.   _____   _____   _____

Answers to the Quiz,

"Your Motivation Quotient"

Following are brief comments that explain the answers to the quiz you have just taken.

1. **Agree.** People who are motivated perform better on the job. People whose work is not very important to them tend to turn in mediocre or inadequate performances.

2. **Disagree.** You cannot really get into the heads of subordinates to know what their attitudes are or whether your efforts to change those attitudes have been successful. Behavior, on the other hand, is recognizable and measurable. You will be less frustrated and more successful if you stick with correcting undesirable or ineffective behavior.

3. **Disagree.** There's no evidence that most people dislike work. In fact, most people would choose meaningful work over idleness or prolonged leisure. There are managers who create working conditions and exhibit styles that subordinates react unfavorably to, and the adverse reaction persuades those same managers that employees really dislike work. It's a vicious, self-fulfilling prophecy.

4. **Disagree.** All human behavior is directed toward a goal. Thus all employees are motivated, are working to achieve something, but that goal may not be what the manager prefers. In such a case, the manager is probably not taking steps to make the work valuable and do-able. The manager who says there is nothing he or she can do is abdicating responsibility and taking the role of a martyr. Neither is satisfying or rewarding.

5. **Not sure.** Some people will work at something they don't like to do, at least for a time. You can't expect them to involve themselves deeply in

it or to be exceptional performers over the long run. It takes too much energy to work at something you don't like for any length of time. However, a manager can take certain steps to persuade people to give their best to a disagreeable task or project on a short-term basis.

6. **Agree.** When people are motivated to commit themselves to working with you toward the achievement of your goals, they are more likely to turn in a good performance than those who are not so committed.

7. **Agree.** Studies have shown that your expectations of employees' work can actually influence that work. If you convey positive expectations—for example, that your subordinates will perform well, they are more likely to do so than if you seem to doubt whether they will. Most people will probably react favorably to a manager who has good feelings and goodwill toward them as people. Furthermore, employees are more likely to accept a manager's guidelines, standards, objectives, and feedback if they know the manager has respect and concern for them.

8. **Disagree.** There is just no scientific evidence that there is a causal relationship between morale and productivity, that low morale results in low motivation. Groups whose morale is low will sometimes turn in high performance. The reverse is also true: Employees whose morale is high will, at times, perform disappointingly. It is probably true that a work group suffering low morale over an extended time will show a decline in productivity, but that has not been substantiated by research.

9. **Disagree.** While most working people value money, there is ample evidence that they do not perform primarily for it. Social psychologist Frederick Herzberg found that mon-

ey is not a motivator. That bears explaining. The promise of more money may have a temporary motivational effect, but the moment an increase is earned, the money ceases to motivate better performance. Furthermore, studies of employee groups through the years show that, while they have an interest in their incomes, money is not as important a motivator as interesting work and the chance for advancement. Money usually appears third or fourth on such lists of motivators or objectives.

10. **Disagree.** If you've ever been subjected to fear from a boss, you'll agree that fear is not a very good way to motivate people. The avoidance of pain or punishment may move people for a short time, but they will eventually come to resent the presence of the stick. Furthermore, they will work to avoid punishment through performance that is minimally acceptable. What enhances the working relationship between manager and employee are respect and credibility. Fear is a poor substitute. And there will be some subordinates who will not experience fear.

11. **Disagree.** Motivation comes from within. You cannot, therefore, motivate anyone but yourself.

12. **Not sure.** No one managerial style can be effective with every employee all the time. Good managers are situational in their approach, altering their styles to fit time, place, conditions, and person. There's no way you can really measure how much a particular style influences motivating factors in employees.

13. **Not sure.** It's nice to be nice to employees, but motivation is considerably more complex than that. Niceness may cause employees to be happy, but not necessarily productive. All we know for sure about happy employees is that they are happy. There are too many other variables to make this premise certain.

14. **Disagree.** Most people welcome criticism if it helps them to work more effectively. No one likes to be a fumbler. No matter how painful criticism may be, it is still less so than failure. Besides, your criticism of employees, constructively put, shows them that you are concerned about their success on the job.

15. **Agree.** People tend to choose the kind of work, task, responsibility, even career, that has the most value and the greater rewards. Thus, before choosing a course of action or a type of behavior, people will want to make sure that the decision will lead to some reward of value.

16. **Agree.** The conditions surrounding the work can make the work harder to do or less possible to complete. Thus the reward for doing the work well becomes more remote, which usually results in lower motivation.

17. **Agree.** People want to be rewarded for doing work, just as they want to achieve something valuable for anything they choose to do. And you have the means to make that work even more rewarding for employees, thus increasing their motivational forces.

18. **Disagree.** Since psychological research shows, overwhelmingly, that most people regard work as essential to their happiness and well-being, there's no reason to believe that they have to be coerced and controlled to make them do a good job. People work to achieve important personal goals. Managers who complain that their employees need to be coerced and controlled have probably created poor working conditions in which people dislike the work, the manager, and/or the environment.

19. **Agree.** It's true that the average employee will not be deeply com-

mitted to a task that he or she doesn't find rewarding to do. That doesn't mean, however, the employee will not do the work. Rather the employee will not be highly motivated over a period of time.

20. **Agree.** Since you are the key to the motivation of your employees—you control the work and the rewards, your managing has much to do with how strongly your employees are motivated.

21. **Agree.** People generally aren't motivated to attempt what they do not believe they can accomplish. If you assign a responsibility to an employee who is doubtful about his or her ability to bring it off, you can expect that the employee will avoid doing the job or will, at least, suffer demotivation. The job may not be done well, if it is done at all.

22. **Agree.** You can often make work more desirable to an employee by adding value to the reward or by making the work easier to do.

23. **Agree.** Given a choice, employees usually won't attempt to do work that doesn't offer some value to them. They may do it if they have no choice; but how well they do it, considering the possibility of their demotivation, is open to question.

24. **Disagree.** Studies of what employees regard as most valuable usually show job security is rather far down on the list. The research of Frederick Herzberg suggests that for most people job security is a "dissatisfier," that is, when people don't have it, they are dissatisfied. But its presence does not act as a motivator. Most employees report that a challenging job with advancement opportunities is much more important to them.

25. **Agree.** You have the ability to increase the value of work in your employees' eyes as well as their confidence in their ability to do it successfully. This chapter will show you how.

Answers to the Internal Reinforcers/Rewards Quiz

1. a, b, c
2. a
3. e
4. a, b, c
5. d
6. e
7. a, c
8. c
9. c, d
10. b, d

Chapter Four

Setting Goals and Measuring Performance

One of the best ways to express your expectations and standards, and to measure performance is through setting goals and using those goals as the basis for appraisals. Goals are natural to people. Aside from the reality that goals determine behavior, they serve a number of needs:

- **Order and structure.** Everyone requires some order and structure in his or her life. Maslow defined these as safety needs, just above food, drink, sleep, and sex.
- **Progress measurement.** People have the need to progress. No one wants to mark time, to stay in the same place. When people recognize and work toward goals, they have a sense of movement.
- **Achievement.** Frederick Herzberg identifies achievement as a motivator. When you set goals and achieve them, you have a sense of accomplishment and satisfaction.
- **Closure.** People like limits: Things have a beginning, middle and an end. Too many open-ended activities can be frustrating, leaving one with the sense of not getting anywhere.
- **Feedback and information.** You need to know where your subordinates are investing their energies and time, and how well they are investing them. A goal is a means of control. You use it to monitor and to adjust performance.

A number of goal-setting programs have not worked. There are several reasons why:

1. **Too many.** There are just so many goals that people can at-

tend to. The danger is that if there are too many goals, none will be reached satisfactorily.

2. **Insufficient accountability.** Some goals are not followed up. Or when they are, and where employees have not achieved, the employees are "forgiven." In either case, the message is, the goals we set don't really count.

3. **Lack of subgoals.** You need to measure progress as you go. You can ill afford to wait for the whole period—six months or a year—to find out what's going on. Or what's not going on. Subgoals show you where you may have to make adjustment—to speed up or slow down, enlarge or scale down. Also, achieving subgoals gives employees a sense of progress that encourages them to work toward completion.

4. **Conflicting priorities.** Once priorities are set, those priorities should be observed unless subsequent events or needs necessitate change. But priorities are to be taken seriously. Frequent changes in priorities create confusion, and possibly even demotivation.

5. **Withholding resources.** Let everyone know that you are a resource to them in their efforts to achieve the goals you have established with them. You have time, knowledge, skill, access to other resources; and you are ready to use them to help employees. You are on the firing line with them.

Kinds and Characteristics of Good Goals

Successful goals that enhance moti-vation have, at least, the following three characteristics: They . . .

. . . are realistic. They offer challenge and a reasonable chance for accomplishment. Set a goal too low, and it loses appeal. Set it too high, and it requires too much risk for most people. One value of setting subgoals is that you can evaluate the degree of risk before it is too late.

. . . are relevant to the organization. Show how a particular goal benefits the organization. Employees can see how their contribution to achievement of the goal affects the well-being of the organization. Employees tend to be less committed to what they consider to be ego goals—something that the manager considers important, but is not essential to the health of the organization. By making sure that goals are relevant, you can avoid the danger that employees will take your goals less seriously than you wish.

. . . relate to the employee. Why is this goal important to the employee? He or she knows what the organization will get from accomplishment of the goal. But how will the personal goals of the employee be achieved through the accomplishment of the organizational goal? The closer you can relate the two, the more commitment you will see in the employee.

In a participative environment, employees expect and need to be part of the goal-setting process. Goals that are simply imposed from the top down may not have strong motivational value. To the extent possible, make the goal-setting process a partnership. And it should be a challenging process. There are four kinds of goals that should be discussed or considered:

● **Routine.** This is an extension of what people are already doing. "Last year you produced 20,000 units; this year, 22,000." "Last period you trained 150; this time you raise the goal to 180." "You've been making fifteen new business calls each week. Try upping that to eighteen." There's some challenge, of course, to improving on the last time period. But if every year a person betters the previous production or output level, he or she comes to expect it. If the goal-setting process consists almost entirely of routine goals, there will be little or no excitement.

While it may be that employees have little to say about the quantity of work to be done, you can give them much to say about how it is to be accomplished. If the new goal is 10 percent higher than the previous one, get their thinking as to how the increase can be achieved.

• **Problem-solving.** Errors are too high. Missed deadlines are too many. The work flow is sluggish. In short, you have a problem. Go to the experts, the people who probably know more about the work than you do. From their counsel, you can set goals with them to solve the problems.

• **Innovation.** Your subordinates are in a knowledgeable position to suggest new and better ways of doing things, or of introducing methods or procedures. In fact, putting some of your best people to work on innovations could be seen as a reward for good performance.

• **Personal.** What are your employees doing for themselves? What kind of training and education, skills building, different behavior, could benefit the employee? What steps could the employee take to advance his or her ability and to become more valuable to the organization? Nothing is more valuable to the employee than his or her personal objectives.

Conducting a Goal-setting Interview

Ideally, your goal-setting interview will be part of the appraising process. Here are the steps to follow:

1. Assemble your records. You'll need the last appraisal and goal-setting records. Collect the documents of any criticism or warnings you may have issued. Compare the goals with actual achievement.

2. Give advance notice. People need time to think about what they regard as important. Unrealistic objectives result when employees have to come up with plans off the top of the head. Suggest that they think about all four kinds of goals that were mentioned previously.

3. Allow plenty of time for the meeting. This is a prime time for the both of you to learn what is on each other's minds. The amount of time you set aside for the process is an indicator of how much importance you assign it. Managers who seem to begrudge the time, who rush through the interview, broadcast that they don't grant much importance to setting goals. This is the opportunity for you to express your expectations and standards. It is also a time for you to make sure that employees have the same perceptions of their jobs that you do.

Employees may bring problems to the session that you were only dimly aware of. They may suggest innovations that you hadn't thought of. And they may furnish you with solid clues as to their personal career objectives, information that you can use in coaching at a later date.

4. Invite the employee to become involved in the process. The worst thing you can do is simply sit there, deliver your evaluation to a silent employee, then terminate the interview. You want to be sure that the employee learns. The appraisal time could also be a learning opportunity for you. The employee may give you feedback that you could find beneficial.

From the outset, make it clear that you want a dialogue, that you don't want to give a speech, that you regard the appraisal process as one of the most important events of the year. One question you can ask is "What's your perception of the quality and quantity of the work you did during the year?"

5. Offer your evaluation. Reinforce the employee's perceptions with your own. Explain where you differ, and why. Your evaluation of the employee will gain more acceptance if you emphasize the positive. Talk about constructive ways the employee can get better results from his or her work.

Your documentation will add credibility to your evaluation. The more objective you are, the more accepting the employee is likely to be.

6. Set new goals. You may want to use the Goal-Setting Data Form on page 89. The statement of the goal, the output not the input, should be followed by:

> Key results of the accomplishment of the goal (how it will be demonstrated and measured);
> The means or input goals, or the plan of action;
> What resources will be available;
> What constraints or limitations will be observed;
> The target date for the accomplishment of the final goal;
> A description of the subgoals with their completion dates;
> The priority rating of the goal;
> The date of the next review.

Each goal requires a separate form. The employee should have a copy of the form for reference during the evaluation period. How much time you spend on the plan of action, on the means of achieving the goal, depends on the complexity of the

goal and the level of proficiency of the employee. With some employees, you'll feel the need to be detailed and explicit. With others you can sketch the outline of the plan and leave the details with them.

7. Get agreement on the goals. Make sure the employee understands the importance of the goal. Every section of the goal-setting form, that is, the resources available to the employee, the limits to what an employee may do to reach the goal, the target or completion dates, the subgoals, should be totally clear. For your part, you can elaborate on how each of the goals relates to your own and the overall organizational goals. Relate each goal to the employee, if possible. How will it contribute to the employee?

Characteristics of Effective Appraisals

One compelling rationale for using goals as the basis for performance evaluation is that it lessens the manager's role as judge, scorekeeper, schoolteacher—all of the roles that make many managers uneasy. Understandably, managers don't like to be seen as sitting in judgment of others or giving marks. When you use goals that you and the employee have agreed on, the two of you, then, agree on the evaluation. You don't have to make guesses or arbitrary decisions. The facts are there, and they are readily acceptable.

Because the goals have been agreed to, and are in writing, there should be no surprises for either of you. What goes on in the appraisal process should be predictable. The employee has essentially the same information you do. If he or she has not been achieving the goals, that information should have been brought to the employee's attention through periodic feedback between appraisals.

Except in the case of failing performance, the appraisal process should produce no more than minimal stress. In fact, employees who are performing well might even look forward to evaluation as confirmation of their own opinions about their work. The chance to relish the achievement of goals, to talk about the future, to set new goals, should be challenging, even exciting.

Should rewards for performance be discussed during evaluation? Probably not. If the employee knows that the type and amount of reward will be announced during the interview, he or she may not listen seriously to the evaluation. It's advisable to make it clear at the outset that there will be no discussion, on this occasion, of rewards. That will come later.

The employee should have some recourse in the event that he disagrees with your assessment. One answer is to permit the employee to submit, in writing, any variance and to file that dissent with the evaluation. That shouldn't happen often. If it does, you'll have to review your appraisal methods. Having a channel for dissent permits the employee to work off some of the negative feelings about the disparity between your perception and the employee's.

The use of goals as the basis for appraisal reduces the possible effect of some common shortcomings in appraising. For example:

• **The halo effect.** Raters may allow one characteristic of an employee to have an excessive influence on their rating of all other factors. For example, the manager appreciates loyalty and may give an employee high ratings in all categories of the evaluation even though the loyal employee's performance is, at best, mediocre.

• **The horns effect.** This has the same lopsidedness as the halo effect, except that it involves a characteristic that the rater dislikes. For example, the manager dislikes the fact that one of his best employees often criticizes the manager to his face. The fact of the employee's outstanding productivity and contributions to the department are rated downward because of the employee's brashness.

• **Leniency and strictness.** Some managers tend to be overly generous in their ratings, often out of fear that they will make a mistake by being too harsh. Some other managers go to the opposite extreme, also in fear of making a mistake, thus rating employees harshly. Excessive leniency or strictness generally stems from differing personal standards.

• **Averaging.** Some evaluators like to play it safe. They avoid placing employees at either the high or low ends. Everyone is clustered in the middle. That way the managers believe they can avoid making errors in judgment and being unfair to anyone. Averaging may also reflect the manager's own standards, against which most employees may be just average performers. Or the managers do a poor job of observing performance as it occurs, and average because they are not sure whether the performance is good or bad.

The performance appraisal is the backbone of a good motivation management system, especially if it is based on the setting and measurement of goals. When goals are involved, you have facts to talk about, not conjecture or opinion. When goals are used as the basis for appraisal, the employee has a continuing, up-to-date answer to the question, "How'm I doing?" The appraisal underlies all five principles of motivation. When you set goals, you tell employees what you expect them to do. By employing goals that are important to employees, you make the work more valuable. Feedback from employees during goal-setting and appraisal helps you to make the job do-able. Appraisal is, of course, the core of your feedback system. Finally, the achievement of the goals at appraisal time shows you whom and what to reward.

Here's a form you might consider using with key subordinates to help them plan job and career progress and to help you in understanding what motivates them. Some executives ask subordinates to fill out both sections, A and B. Employees are to retain Section A for themselves. The executives retain Section B, which translates those goals into specific on-the-job actions. They can also use this portion of the form as a basis for coaching employees on their progress.

Personal Goals Inventory

Section A

In the following spaces, write down those personal goals that you would like to achieve through your work. As a thought-starter, would you like to achieve money, a promotion, a specific kind of responsibility, esteem of others in the organization or in your profession, a sense of professional growth, more freedom in your work or schedule, etc.? List everything that you can identify as a motivating force in you.

_____

_____

_____

_____

_____

_____

_____

_____

_____

Section B

Review your entries and rank them according to priority. In the blank spaces below, translate the most important of the personal goals-motivating factors you listed above into specific actions you can take, or would like to take, on the job in the next five years in order to achieve them.

For example, if you are motivated, among other things, by professional recognition, what actions can you take to achieve it through your work? You might qualify for membership in a professional organization and become active. You might write an article. You might take courses or qualify for a certificate. Look at on-the-job opportunities for you to increase your professional expertise and standing.

If you want more responsibility, what path can you plot that would lead you to it? What training would help?

Write down specific job and career strategies that would help you to achieve the goals you listed:

_____   _____

_____   _____

_____   _____

_____   _____

_____   _____

_____   _____

Goal-Setting Data Form

1. Name of employee: _____

_____

2. Statement of output or final goal: _____

_____

_____

_____

_____

_____

3. Key results of the accomplishment of the goal (how measured):

    a. _____

    _____

    _____

    b. _____

    _____

    _____

c. _____

_____

_____

4. Means, input goals, plan of action: _____

_____

_____

_____

_____

_____

_____

_____

_____

5. Resources available: _____

_____

_____

_____

_____

_____

_____

6. Constraints or limitations to be observed: _____

_____

_____

_____

_____

_____

_____

_____

7. Target date for accomplishment of goal: _____

8. Description of subgoals, if any, and dates for accomplishment:

    a. _____ Date: _____

    b. _____ Date: _____

    c. _____ Date: _____

    d. _____ Date: _____

9. Priority rating of goal: _____

10. Date of review: _____

I have read the above and agree with the action plan and the goal to be achieved.

                            _____

                               (Employee's signature)

                         Date of agreement: _____

Chapter Five

Upgrading the Effectiveness of Your Work Group

American managers have often been criticized for their preoccupation with the short-term bottom line. Whether or not that is an unnecessarily harsh judgment, there is no question that many managers, although conscious of the need to continually upgrade the effectiveness of their employees, put it off or do it in a haphazard fashion.

Times change. Working conditions change. The business environment changes. Your employees will be called on to demonstrate sharper or new skills, to be more adaptable and responsive, to be more confident in their ability to meet the contingencies that arise and can't always be anticipated. While many employees will take it upon themselves to acquire the knowledge and training that will equip them to deal with change, **you** are the key to upgrading the effectiveness of all your subordinates. You occupy a vantage

point. Generally speaking, you have access to more information and resources. You have a better view of what your organization needs and what it has to offer employees. You have the authority to institute training, new procedures, and to eliminate outdated ways of doing things. If you are a true leader, you also have vision, a sense of direction, and the power to inspire your subordinates.

There are five chief approaches to helping your employees through the change process:

1. Managing the change process itself and gaining acceptance of it;
2. Pushing responsibility down through delegation;
3. Taking responsibility for training;
4. Coaching employees; and
5. Managing conflict.

93

All five approaches constitute a positive process although an unwitting manager can make some of them negative. For example, you often hear managers complain that their employees resist change. In fact, most people can be stimulated by change and new challenges. They do tend to resist changes they perceive to be unpleasant, threatening, or otherwise disadvantageous to them. Training is an example of a positive experience that is often viewed as a minus, if only because many employees have experienced training as an antidote for their "deficiencies" or as a waste of time. People who are trained in new methods and skills and who are not permitted to practice them grow disillusioned with the training process.

All five approaches have growth potential. But to keep the experience positive, you must take steps to allay employees' anxieties as well as your own. You must work to build their confidence in their ability to function effectively. Otherwise, they will experience demotivation and you will suffer from their drop in productivity.

Managing Change

People are not automatically resistant to change. They are, however, understandably, resistant to what they fear is being done to them. Thus, when you have to announce and explain a forthcoming change to your people, say enough to them to overcome their fears. Remember that they will be asking questions such as these:

- What does this mean to the organization? Are we growing or retrenching?
- How does it affect my future? Will it help me or hurt me?

- Does the change imply any criticism of me (or employees in general)? Do we get blamed for the factors that led to the change?
- What can I lose as a result of the change? Money, prestige, advancement?
- How does it affect the people around me? Will it change my work group? Will some people get ahead of me?
- Will it make me look good or bad?

Anticipating such questions and fears will help you to allay some of the anxieties. Managers often make unnecessary trouble for themselves when they overlook the need to uncover such frequently unvoiced anxieties. Even if some of the answers are negative or unpleasant, it's better to get the facts out in the open rather than have employees' suspicions fester. The grapevine will feed on those suspicions.

When you have to introduce change that you suspect will be unpopular, such as more complicated procedures, transfers of responsibility, or an increased work load, reduce the trauma as much as possible. Here are some recommendations you'll want to follow:

- **Convey positive expectations.** Indicate that you have weighed the pros and cons and have decided that, despite drawbacks, that good will come out of the change. People's expectations about a change can significantly affect its success. When you express doubts or show that you expect subordinates to be disturbed, you pave the way for problems. But if you can show some optimism, the change becomes less threatening.
- **Don't knock the status quo.** You may be tempted to say something

such as "Things are so bad now that we're forced to change." Before you do, remember that some of your people may have been instrumental in bringing things to their current state. If you are especially critical of the current operation, you'll wind up antagonizing those whose support you want.

- **Anticipate fears.** Bring the objections you anticipate into the open. Otherwise, they may fester and cause problems later. Ask for comments and questions about the change. If you know of objections that are not brought up, mention them yourself and provide answers. As much as possible, give the reasons for the change and try to emphasize its positive aspects. Even an across-the-board pay cut or reduction in force has some virtues compared to shutting down the operation.

- **Accept the fears.** There may be some emotional reactions to the change that can't be explained away or buried by rational explanations. Sometimes, after you've exhausted the explanations, you'll find that negative reactions persist. There may be little you can do but accept them. Don't imply to the employees that they have no right to their feelings. Your acceptance of them will go a long way toward calming the fears. Your denial of them will simply stiffen resistance.

- **Get people involved.** The nearly ideal solution in making change and reducing resistance is to get people involved in the original planning for the change. "We have this need (or this problem). What do you think we ought to do about it?" But if that isn't possible, try to give people a voice in the implementation of the change. If subordinates can be involved in planning how the change will be carried out, they are more likely to accept it. The hardest changes to get accepted are those that come completely packaged, with no room for discussion.

- **Use a trial run.** Introducing a change on a trial basis avoids making it seem as if you are ramming something down people's throats. Six months from now, everyone may be sold on its value. Or you may have experimented and found that another way is better. It's seldom that your original plan can't be improved on.

It bears repeating: In making a change, try whenever possible to involve your employees in the planning stage. If they can develop some ownership in the project, their resistance will be lessened and their commitment will be intensified.

Employees' paranoia during times of change is real and needs to be dealt with. And the paranoia is especially heavy when changes are in the wind and employees do not feel sufficiently informed. Perhaps, because the change is coming from above, you can't close the information gap completely, but you can cut down on the paranoia. And you have good reason to do so. When people are anxious, they spend much time and energy talking among themselves, worrying and speculating, often outlandishly. This can detract from productivity. Here are some steps you can take:

- **Tell what you can.** You may not know much more than the people who report to you, but share what you can with them. Because of your position, your knowledge of the operation, and your own grapevine, you are bound to have more information than people on levels below you.

- **Encourage employees to ask questions.** You may not know the answers. If not, let them know you don't. Otherwise they will suspect that you are hiding the truth, and they will conclude that it means bad news for them.

Their questions serve other purposes: First, they let you know what is being voiced, and sometimes those questions will reflect very wild speculation. You'll probably be able to quash extreme rumors. Second, they give you solid evidence with which to approach higher management and say, "Here's what people are worrying themselves with." You may get answers to some of the specific questions. You can then take the information back.

● **Increase your contacts.** Make yourself more visible and accessible during a crisis or a period when employees show anxiety. Some managers, feeling somewhat anxious themselves, or helpless, spend more time behind closed doors. Their isolation only increases the tension in the atmosphere. Walk around. Chat. Be seen. Even though you cannot allay all the fears, your presence is a steadying force.

● **Don't try to put on a happy face.** If you sense that things are serious, don't, for the sake of morale, try to pretend otherwise. You don't have to be dour—and you shouldn't be, but you cannot afford to be falsely cheerful, as if nothing bad is going on. When the truth is known, you will lose respect and credibility. Further, you will appear uncaring.

In times of change, employees view you as part of management, the "they" from whom the changes are coming. You have a chance to become part of the "we" by showing your concern for employees, by attending to their needs as much as possible. And you may do a favor for higher management by helping them to become less of "they" and more of "we" by your serving as a channel of communication, up and down.

Increasing the Effectiveness of Subordinates through Delegating

From the time you first became a manager, you have heard the word: Delegate. It's easy to preach; it's not so easy to practice. For one thing, delegation takes planning, and you are busy. You probably keep telling yourself that you'll lay out a number of delegatable tasks next week, and prepare employees for them. But next week comes and goes, and you're still busy.

Another reason why managers find delegating difficult is that there is a lot of risk involved. As manager, you're still responsible for whatever you pass along to your subordinates. If they foul up an assignment, you have to pick up the pieces. There's always the temptation not to delegate, not to take the risk. Many managers believe in the old dictum, "If you want the job done right, do it yourself."

And a third reason for hesitating to delegate is that you may worry about an adverse reaction from employees who feel that you are overloading them. You are giving them more work, more responsibility, without paying them more.

But there are pressing reasons *why* you must delegate. For example, if you are working long hours, consider your personal needs. What about your health? Your family life? Your recreational needs? And your intellectual growth needs? You need time to think and reflect, to occupy yourself with concerns other than business.

No doubt your job is changing. More responsibility is being pushed down on you from above. You have to balance that new pressure by getting rid of some of your tasks, tasks that others can do. You should concentrate on those responsibilities that only you can discharge—planning, budgeting, allocation of resources, generating new ideas to push up the line, etc. If you are burdened with old tasks that you have been performing for a long time, you're going to be less effective in those areas in which you are being evaluated.

Finally, if you continue to do the same tasks and routines year after year, your job is going to be less and less enjoyable. And you'll have to ask yourself whether you surround yourself with the familiar to avoid having to undertake the new. It's usually a sign of obsolescence, and you definitely don't want to have the feeling that you are becoming obsolete. That doesn't help your self-esteem. And it certainly doesn't present a good image to others.

If your subordinates continue to do what they've been doing for a long time, their jobs also become less enjoyable and satisfying. It's estimated that 80 percent of most jobs can be learned in two to three years. If people continue to do essentially the same thing after that, it means they are in an overlearning situation. They spend the next several years learning the other 20 percent, which is hardly efficient. Their growth is slowed. And growth, you'll recall from Herzberg, is a motivator. When it slows down, so does motivation.

There is at least one other argument for enriching the jobs of your employees through delegation. If you manage a work group that does not increase its effectiveness on a continuing basis, you are, in effect, managing regressively. The world is changing. The work environment is changing. Yet, your people do not. Keep them effective by giving them responsibilities that require change and growth.

How Are You As a Delegator?

To determine your need to delegate, answer the following questions as candidly as you can.

	Yes	No
1. Do you take work home often, more often than other managers with comparable responsibilities?	_____	_____
2. Do you regularly work longer hours than the people you manage?	_____	_____
3. Do you spend part of your day doing tasks that employees ask your help on or that they could probably do on their own?	_____	_____
4. Do you lack confidence in the abilities of any of your subordinates, which makes you reluctant to delegate to them?	_____	_____
5. Are there tasks that you would like to delegate but have not because you have not wished to take the time to instruct the subordinate?	_____	_____

	Yes	No

6. Have you decided not to delegate tasks to subordinates because you suspected you might end up spending more time monitoring than if you went ahead and did it yourself? _____ _____

7. Are you reluctant to take your full vacation time because you worry about your department's being able to operate well in your absence? _____ _____

8. Do you admit to yourself that you are a perfectionist on details, large and small? _____ _____

9. Do you frequently hesitate to delegate to subordinates because you fear they will not perform the work as conscientiously as you would like? _____ _____

10. When you return from an absence, have matters that subordinates thought needed your attention piled up? _____ _____

11. Do you feel that your authority enables you to undertake more work or requires you to have a greater sense of responsibility than your subordinates could achieve? _____ _____

12. Do you believe it is impossible to delegate to your subordinates because they are just too busy? _____ _____

13. Do many of your employees perform essentially the same kinds of duties year in, year out? _____ _____

14. Do you have good performers who often seem bored with their jobs or complain about the sameness of their responsibilities? _____ _____

15. Do some of your employees suggest to you from time to time that they would welcome more challenge? _____ _____

16. Do you observe your supervisors performing tasks that, in your opinion, they could delegate to their subordinates? _____ _____

17. Do you frequently suggest to employees to whom you have delegated tasks that you will do the finishing up? _____ _____

18. Is your usual reaction to articles and talks on delegation that your situation is different from what the speakers or writers describe? _____ _____

If you are a frequent delegator, you will probably score no more than five *yes* answers. Nonetheless, look at those questions that you have answered in the affirmative to see where you might do some fine-tuning.

If you answered more than five questions with *yes*, no one needs to point out that you are a reluctant or an infrequent delegator. Your reluctance to delegate and anxious feelings about doing it are not different from the way most managers feel about delegation. But if you are to have an effective work team, indeed if you are to be effective yourself, you will have to start pushing down some of your responsibilities. The recommendations in this section of the book will help you to build confidence in your ability to delegate and in employees' abilities to perform the work according to your standards.

Following are some recommendations for delegating for maximum results:

• **Don't limit delegation to proven performers.** If you distribute assignments to everyone, you build a team of versatile performers, a handy group to have when crises or emergencies arise. You may be tempted because of work and time pressure to pick the people you know you can rely on. But in doing so, you risk demotivating others and overloading your key people, which, ironically, may also result in their demotivation.

• **Select assignments that stretch, but won't break.** Remember that confidence in being able to do the task is necessary for motivation. Don't create an immoderate risk by giving people assignments they worry about being able to handle. The last thing in the world you want is for them to fail.

• **Match the assignment to the individual.** From what you know of the employee, his or her abilities and interests, what can you assign that will

have a motivating effect? If the job itself is not terribly interesting or challenging, what kind of reward could you offer for its successful completion? Think about both internal **and** external rewards.

• **Make sure employees know what they must do.** When you delegate, ask open-ended questions to get detailed responses. Don't ask an employee whether he or she understands the assignment. That will often give you a *yes* answer with little or no further information. Instead, ask how they think the job can best be done, what is entailed, how long it will take, and what they think the final results will be.

• **Vary your coaching techniques.** Some employees will need only a brief discussion of what will be required to carry out a new type of assignment. Others may need periodic guidance over the period of the assignment.

• **Give subordinates the responsibility and authority to carry out the job.** Part of your job when delegating is to explain and to demonstrate. The rest is to leave subordinates alone to carry out the assignment in their own way. If an individual asks for help later—or if it becomes obvious that help is needed—resist the temptation to provide a complete answer, methodology, or a detailed procedure. Instead, help people to think through problems, to find their own solutions. You don't want to be seen as an automatic rescuer when subordinates encounter the slightest difficulties. Nor do you want to be perceived as dictating the way tasks are done. No one will find much challenge in taking on assignments under such conditions.

Staying in Control

No matter how often or how much

you delegate, you're bound to feel somewhat nervous when delegating an important task. After all, you don't give up responsibility, and you don't have to give up all control. Be honest with employees about your anxious feelings. Be as positive as possible. And be available.

• **Anxieties.** When you delegate, arrange for periodic reports and consultations. Explain to the employee that you are especially concerned about delegating this responsibility. If you set up a reporting and checking schedule at the outset, the employee is less likely to interpret that as negative feedback from you than if you imposed such a schedule after the work has started. The subordinate should get the message that if the work goes well, your anxieties will abate, and so will your need to have frequent reports. Clearly communicate that the best way to work with you on this task is to keep you apprised, at least in the early stages.

• **Stay positive.** Make your checkups in a positive manner. For example, "Terry, when Sam Whittaker completed a similar assignment a couple of years ago, he wrote a report suggesting ways it might have been done better." You can make it clear that the employee has the choice of whether to use Sam's recommendations or not. If you don't have anything quite so elaborate as a postmortem on a previous assignment, make up your own. You can always say, "When I used to handle this, one of the concerns I had was . . ." If the employee is making progress on the work, she'll probably not be uneasy about your expression of interest, especially if you leave it up to her whether she wants to incorporate your or Sam's thinking. She'll probably feel encouraged to discuss any possible difficulties without feeling threatened or smothered.

• **Availability.** If you show that you're willing to supply information or have a discussion with a subordinate about the work in progress, he or she will tend to come to you. Make sure the employee knows that you are there as a resource to be consulted.

Here are some other steps you can take to reduce your feeling of risk and anxieties:

• **Assign only preliminaries.** You are studying a problem or considering a new project. You're not sure you are ready to entrust the assignment to a subordinate. But why not ask a subordinate to make a study or gather information? You can also ask him or her to make recommendations at the conclusion of the study. Then you can decide whether you want to delegate the principal task.

• **Give out parts of jobs.** Break a task into segments, and farm the segments out. You spread the risk. For example, you're thinking about introducing flexible working hours. That may be a big chunk of work for one subordinate. Instead, let one employee research types of flexible schedules. Another can study the preferences of individuals for work schedules.

• **Keep control of the task until you feel the subordinate is ready to take over.** Let the employee know at the outset that you will retain control or final approval until the employee and you develop confidence in his or her ability to do the work without heavy monitoring. Let up as it becomes obvious that the subordinate can handle the responsibility and feels secure in doing so.

• **Be prepared to coach as often as necessary.** Remember that a key coaching technique is to encourage the subordinate to think and come up with answers. Thus, avoid the temptation to give a quick, sound answer. Ask questions such as: "What are the factors you consider most important in this situation?" "What options do you have?" "What are the pluses and minuses of the option you've chosen?" "Do you think you could use more information before you decide?"

What and When to Delegate

Use the following questionnaires to help you identify tasks that you can delegate and employees to whom they are delegatable.

Inventory of Delegatable Tasks

List the tasks that . . .
1. You do because you like to do them:

a. _____   _____

b. _____   _____

c. _____   _____

d. _____   _____

e. _____   _____

f. _____   _____

g. _____   _____

NOTE: Place a check after each task that could be performed by a subordinate now.

2. You held on to when you had your last promotion, that you brought upward with you.

a. _____   _____

b. _____   _____

c. _____   _____

d. _____   _____

e. _____   _____

f. _____   _____

g. _____   _____

NOTE: Once again, place a check after each task that could be performed at your former level of authority.

3. Have become sufficiently routine that some of your subordinates can do them:

    a. _____

    b. _____

    c. _____

    d. _____

    e. _____

    f. _____

    g. _____

4. You formerly liked to do, but no longer find interesting or challenging:

    a. _____

    b. _____

    c. _____

    d. _____

    e. _____

    f. _____

    g. _____

5. Subordinates ask your help on frequently:

    a. _____

    b. _____

    c. _____

    d. _____

    e. _____

    f. _____

    g. _____

6. Cause you to work long hours or contribute substantially to your work load.

a. _____

Components that might be delegated to others:

_____

_____

_____

_____

b. _____

Components that might be delegated to others:

_____

_____

_____

_____

c. _____

Components that might be delegated to others:

_____

_____

_____

_____

d. _____

Components that might be delegated to others:

_____

_____

_____

_____

7. You would delegate if you had more confidence in the abilities of your subordinates or time to instruct them properly:

a. _____

b. _____

c. _____

d. _____

List subordinates potentially capable of taking on the above tasks, and action plans to prepare them:

Employee: _____

Action plan: _____

_____

_____

Date of completion of action plan: _____

Employee: _____

Action plan: _____

_____

_____

Date of completion of action plan: _____

Employee: _____

Action plan: _____

_____

_____

Date of completion of action plan: _____

Employee: _____

Action plan: _____

_____

_____

Date of completion of action plan: _____

8. Usually pile up in your absence.

a. _____

Employee capable of handling it: _____

Instructions next time: _____

_____

_____

b. _____

Employee capable of handling it: _____

Instructions next time: _____

_____

_____

c. _____

Employee capable of handling it: _____

Instructions next time: _____

_____

_____

d. _____

Employee capable of handling it: _____

Instructions next time: _____

_____

_____

9. WORK-LOAD DISTRIBUTION. On the left, make a list of key employees to whom you might delegate tasks if they were not already very busy. In the center, identify some of their present responsibilities that could be distributed among other subordinates. On the right, list employees who are capable of assuming the distributed responsibilities.

Key People	Tasks	Recipients
_____	_____	_____
	_____	_____
	_____	_____
_____	_____	_____
	_____	_____
	_____	_____
_____	_____	_____
	_____	_____
_____	_____	_____
	_____	_____
_____	_____	_____
	_____	_____
	_____	_____
_____	_____	_____
	_____	_____

10. Have you observed your supervisors performing tasks that you believe they could delegate to their subordinates?

Supervisor	Task	Subordinate
_____	_____	_____
	_____	_____
	_____	_____
_____	_____	_____
	_____	_____
	_____	_____
_____	_____	_____
	_____	_____
	_____	_____

Be especially alert to the opportunities to delegate when you are away from the office. Not only does delegation at this time tell employees that they may be more self-starting and that you want them to assume more responsibility, but you also reduce tension and worry among them as to how matters should be handled in your absence. Some steps for you to consider:

1. **Prepare a list of problems that might arise in your absence.** You have a fair idea of what might happen, although you can't anticipate every contingency.
2. **Arrange with subordinates to handle these problems as they arise.** Make explicit assignments and grant authority. You may want to make the assignments in writing so that there is no question about someone's having the authority.
3. **Make sure your assistant or some other key person knows of all the assignments.** As contingencies occur, someone should know where to field them. Also, there should be someone your subordinates should consult if they have questions about the assignments, resources, constraints, etc.
4. **Provide necessary information for each assignee.** Don't leave valuable data locked in your desk where it is inaccessible, or hidden in a file where no one knows to look.

Taking Responsibility for Training

You are the key to employees' growth. You know your employees. You know what they need to learn: technical or administrative skills, management methods, problem-solving or decision-making techniques, conflict management, computer literacy, etc. More important, you can see that they apply their new knowledge and skills in a supportive, reinforcing environment.

Much training on the corporate scene is inefficient. The value for each dollar spent is too low. There are several reasons for this. Often the content of training is dictated by higher management or, in some cases, by the human resource people. Their perceptions of your training needs might not be yours. Another problem is that much training takes place in an artificial environment: a classroom away from the work scene. The conditions under which the trainee learns are often not similar to those under which he or she works. The learning takes place in a vacuum. The learner does not always see the relevance of the material. In some cases, there is little or no relevance. But the most frequent inhibitor to learning and training is the lack of application and reinforcement back on the job.

To illustrate, a supervisor enrolls in a workshop on participative management skills or interpersonal competence. But when she gets back to the job, she finds that the boss really isn't much interested in what she learned. He has his own style, his own way of doing things. He doesn't encourage her to practice what she's learned. His response is probably along the lines of "That is fine for the classroom, but this is the real world." In many other cases, people get busy and absorbed and just don't apply the learning because no one encourages them to. The training is soon forgotten.

You can exercise a positive influence on the training of your people. You can work with your training department, or with an outside training consultant if you don't have internal specialists to diagnose your training needs. You can then work with the specialist to make sure that the training program satisfies those needs; that it focuses on the kinds of skills and knowledge that are important to your operation. Finally, you help the trainee look for ways to apply the new knowledge and skills on the job, and then reinforce or reward the application.

There will be times when you will not use a trainer. You, in fact, will be the trainer, or one of your employees will perform the role. Much of the training that goes on may be informal, on the job, outside a classroom. You must accept the major part of the responsibility for keeping your employees in a growth environment. You need to know, consequently, how adults learn. Their learning is quite different from how children learn. Very often, the pattern in children's education is to stuff knowledge into them. Children are not always shown why they are learning something. They know what they are expected to do if they are to avoid penalties. But adults need reasons. The motivation to learn is very similar to the motivation to do anything else. Here are some considerations concerning adult learning:

A reason for learning. It is not enough to say, "I want you to take a course in public speaking." You may have a reason that is valuable for you, but it may not carry much value for the employee. Another approach might be, "I've noticed in meetings that you are very articulate. We have some presentations that have to be made regarding the new X-10 line when it comes out the first of the year. We have to educate our own people on the technical and marketing aspects, and since you do so well in meetings, I'm sure you would be a good spokesman for us. And of course, you'd get a lot of visibility in the company." If the employee finds that prospect a challenge, then you have an eager learner.

Your assurances. You might have to persuade the employee that he or she has the ability to learn the new skill. How many times have you observed the employee display a talent for the work, however undeveloped? You might say, "I'm selecting you for the training because I think you'd find it useful. And I'm convinced that you have a knack for it. You seem to work fast and well with numbers, and some quantitative decision-making methods would be good for the department." People may have some hesitation about taking on something new until you demonstrate that you've observed them showing some of the talent or the potential already, that the training won't involve something new and strange to them after all.

A chance to apply. Employees in learning situations need opportunities to practice. This completes and reinforces the learning. One of the biggest drawbacks to learning away from the work situation is that there is a time gap between the learning and the doing. During that gap, some of the learning is lost. Arrange for a quick application and repetition of the new skill.

Feedback. "How am I doing?" is a question to which everyone wants the answer. It is just as important in the learning process as it is in any other aspect of motivation. Not only do you provide the chance for the employee to practice or to apply the new knowledge or skill, you provide guidance and support through feedback. The more positive your feedback is, the better.

If your trainee is going out of the department for the training, meet with him or her to help set learning objectives. What would the subordi-nate like to come back with in the way of skills and knowledge? What do you believe some of the learning objectives should be? The value of this exercise is to prime the subordinate for the training session, to get him or her in a learning mode, and to look for ways he or she can achieve the objectives during the training.

After the training is complete, hold another session with the employee to discuss the objectives and how well they were attained. Then look for assignments and duties that will help the employee reinforce the training.

When the application is successful, recognize it. Once the new knowledge is well established, reinforce it intermittently.

Coaching Employees

When you coach employees, you work with them to develop their potential skills and to sharpen the skills they are practicing today. There are two kinds of coaching: short-term and long-term.

Short-term coaching is problem-centered, whereas long-term coaching is oriented to the growth and development of the employee. When an employee comes to you with a problem that is preventing full effectiveness on the job, you coach the employee through the process of developing alternative answers and selecting the one that may solve the problem. Long-term coaching, for growth, is a process you usually initiate.

Managers typically pay more attention to the problem-centered situation, because the problem provides a barrier to productivity. It is a fire that must be extinguished. Because they are busy fighting fires, these managers tend to procrastinate on the long-term coaching obligation. But if you are to have an effectively functioning work force tomorrow, you cannot afford to neglect the growth and development coaching today.

Problem-Centered Coaching

In problem-centered coaching, some or all of the following procedures may be helpful.

1. Get agreement that a problem exists. You may have your own opinion on the nature of the problem and how it developed. And you may assume that the other person sees the problem from your perspective. That may not be necessarily true. It's possible that the subordinate does not recognize the problem at all. Or does not share your perception of the seriousness of the problem. Take time to establish an agreement on the problem at the outset, otherwise your coaching could be wasted. Perhaps more serious is the gap between what the subordinate regards as a problem and what you see as one. The existence of that gap could indicate some fundamental differences in values and standards between the two of you.

Stick with behavior in describing the problem. You may have some theories about why the deficiency occurs. But that is speculation; behavior is not.

Don't rush to a solution. It's not a good idea to insist that subordinates bring a solution along with the problem because if they can't come up with a solution, they may not tell you about the problem. Your coaching will help the subordinate to generate options and select the one most suitable.

2. Define the various options.
Think of what you'd prefer to see as an alternative to the situation or the problem that exists. Correcting a problem may do little more than bring you back to where you were. An alternative may bring correction and improvement. Do not be in a hurry to settle on an option until you're reasonably sure that you have developed as many options as you can.

Go easy on the "Who's to blame for this?" It's better to say, "What has happened?" It's far better to say, "What would be preferable?" When a subordinate suspects you are primarily interested in fixing blame, he or she will get defensive, and you'll have a more difficult time getting necessary information.

3. Define the preferred as a goal. You'll need some standards and measurements. Progress can be measured as behavior change, units of output, new competence. Goals should be set in a time frame; and you'll probably want subgoals to let you know you're making progress.

4. Have a Plan B. Your original selection, no matter how well-intentioned and thought out, may have to be scrapped or modified. So know when and how you may have to intervene, either to point the subordinate in a different direction or to take corrective action yourself.

5. Determine your role. Should you provide authority? Training reassignment? What counseling or feedback may be desirable? Should your presence be direct or indirect? Get your subordinate to understand the role you plan to play.

6. Set up a program of review. Once you've determined a plan of action, you should review it from time to time to make sure it's working. It's best to establish a schedule of review in advance so that no one forgets it should be done—and the subordinate doesn't feel that you're meddling.

7. Give feedback. If the subordinate isn't following the plan, he or she should know. If the subordinate is succeeding, he or she needs to know that, too.

Short-term coaching is not restricted to problems. A subordinate may come to you with an idea or a project, or may come to you for help on a decision. Such requests deserve coaching by you. Your role is the same as if you were dealing with a problem: help the subordinate to define the situation and to generate options, to evaluate the options, and to set goals. You must also decide on your role, review progress if necessary, and give feedback.

The emphasis in coaching is on the development of your people. It isn't enough to help them find a solution or make a decision. Through your coaching, they should also be able to study how that solution or decision is arrived at. Eventually they'll be able to act on their own.

A Problem-Centered Coaching Scenario

You are a national sales manager. In looking over the monthly summaries of salespeople's activity, you note that one of your most experienced, achieving salespeople has been in a decline for several months. Each month Harry's volume has been slightly less than it was the previous month. It shows a pattern that you are concerned about. You call Harry's field manager on the phone to discuss the steady decline. You suspect Harry's manager, whose name is Jim, could use some coaching, because Jim has been a manager only about six months.

You: Hi, Jim. I thought perhaps you and I ought to have a chat about Harry. Each month he's doing less and less.
Jim: He's still one of our top people, though.
You: Well, not if he keeps this up.
Jim: It's possible, Art, that this is just a temporary thing. I talked with him on the phone, and he seems all right. I mean, I didn't get any clues that he's in a slump.
You: So you think there's no problem?
Jim: Well, nothing serious, I'd say.
You: But suppose you're optimistic, too optimistic. Suppose after three more months of a fall-off in volume, we have a real problem that we can't ignore. It's going to be a lot tougher to turn around. Sure you want to take the chance?
Jim: If you're convinced we ought to move, I guess we should.
You: Let me put it another way. For the past ten years, Harry has usually increased his volume every month, maybe not by much, but it's been a steady increase. Now we have a steady decrease for four months running. What do you think?
Jim: It could be the first stages of a problem. I agree. What do you think I ought to do about it? You've known Harry for years.
You: Let's see what the options might be.

Wisely, you don't proceed to talk about solutions before you obtain Jim's agreement that a problem indeed exists with Harry. Furthermore, you toss the options ball back to Jim. It's not unusual for the subordinate in a coaching situation to ask the boss to supply a solution. To do so would defeat the purpose of coaching.

Jim: One option might be early retirement.
You: Yes, but why do you suggest that?
Jim: I have a theory about Harry. He's close to sixty. His kids are grown and out of college. He's made a lot of money. Maybe he's slowing down, getting ready to retire.
You: Has he said anything like that to you?
Jim: No.
You: Early retirement is a possibility. But why do you suppose his decline is only for the last four months? Have you worked with him during that time?
Jim: Art, I haven't worked with Harry at all. I've been attending to the trouble spots. As you know, Marian has been in big trouble. I just don't think she'll make it. And I've had the two new men. I've had to spend quite a bit of time with them. Harry just didn't seem to demand my time.
You: You have tended to the squeaky wheels?
Jim: Right.
You: There might be a clue.
Jim: You think he's upset because I haven't worked with him?
You: Look at it this way. Say you are Harry. You've been number one in the district for a long time. A new manager takes over, and doesn't take time to come see you. How would you feel?
Jim: I might feel grateful that I was being left alone. Then again, maybe I might believe no one much cared.

Asking questions at this point in the coaching sequence is a good tech-nique for encouraging your subordinate to think through the various aspects of the problem and to develop possible options. The information that you can help the subordinate generate is of more value to him or her because it is the subordinate's thinking. There's a certain amount of ownership involved.

You: Which do you think might be more likely?
Jim: I don't know. The point is, I haven't been to see him, and I probably should.
You: If you spend some time with him, you may develop a better understanding of what's going on. At any rate, investing time in your top salesman can't be considered a waste.
Jim: You're right. He wasn't having trouble, so he wasn't high priority. I wonder if that's what he felt?

Jim has made a mistake common to many managers. He goes where the wheel squeaks. He is right that his job is to increase the effectiveness of his salespeople. But if he invests his time helping people who are already producing well to increase their productivity, the return from his investment of time will be much greater than a similar amount of time spent with a poor or mediocre salesperson. That's not to say that he can afford to overlook the disappointing producers. Rather he cannot afford to overlook the people who already do a good job.

You: You'll find out when you visit. Harry's a pretty upfront guy. He'll clue you in. How do you plan to approach Harry on the drop in volume?

Jim: I'll show him. He can tell me what's wrong, if anything is.

You: Suppose he lets you know that he plans to take it easy from now on.

Jim: No way. If he wants to do that, he should retire. Or if he wants to stay on, we can cut his territory and I can put another person in there and do fine.

You: What are some other possibilities? Suppose he's bored? It happens. People go on and on, and then realize that it's getting old hat.

Jim: He has to sell if he's going to keep the territory.

You: Let's think about how else we might get value from him.

Jim: There is one thing.

You: Yeah?

Jim: I could sure use help in training. Do you suppose he could do that?

You: He might. And he might just like it.

Jim: One other thought. If he doesn't want to work as hard as he used to, I could ask him to share the territory with a younger person. Harry could keep some of the accounts and train the other person to take over the rest. That way, when Harry does retire, we'd have someone to step in.

You: Now you're thinking. So what's your main approach?

Just by continuing to ask questions and to suggest that there might be other possibilities, you've succeeded in getting Jim to develop a number of options. Now it's time to put priorities on them.

Jim: Well, if he's going to keep the territory as it is, he has to produce quota. He's fallen under that.

You: Should we require that he immediately get back to quota?

Jim: I'll tell him he has to finish the year on quota. So that'll give him a little time to rebuild momentum.

You: And if he's not interested?

Jim: Then I'll suggest one of the other options—a partner, cutting the territory, working with me on training.

You: Good. You've got fallback positions. When are you going to see Harry?

Jim: Next week. I'll call him as soon as I get off the phone with you.

You: Anything you need from me?

Jim: No. Just your support later for the changes we've discussed if we have to go that route.

Jim now has a goal, a time frame, and some options in case Harry does not want to fill his quota. Much of the thinking was done by Jim, which is the way it should be in a coaching session. The manager's job in coaching is to stimulate and guide that thinking, then tie down the plan of action.

Coaching for Growth

Developing your people resources for the long haul is an essential part of your job. You accept that. Yet, you are busy. Other, more immediate concerns tend to push aside the coaching function. To counteract this tendency, you might consider following the recommendations below:

● **Schedule periodic coaching sessions.** If you don't, you risk letting your fire-fighting activity crowd this obligation out. You should certainly plan at least one coaching session with each employee during the year, perhaps two, especially in the case of fast trackers.

• **Set up a data bank.** Take notes during the interview or immediately after. Otherwise you'll forget some of the areas covered. Many times, a scrap of conversation or a bit of information gleaned indirectly will alert you to a quality you never knew the person had.

• **Present specific guidelines.** "Growth and development" is an amorphous phrase. And this may be another reason why many managers have difficulty in coming to grips with it. Giving shape to a growth and development program is a job that requires managerial imagination—and precision. Discussions with the subordinate should point to specific developmental experiences such as further training and education, a field trip, servicing a key account, temporary duty in another department, a new assignment, reading. These suggestions should become part of your notes.

• **Update your information.** Follow up on your suggestions to see whether progress has been made. You may well discover that the employee has come a significant ways in developing a new skill or sharpening an old one since your last coaching session. Check on the validity of old data. What the employee said two years ago—for example, expressing that he wasn't interested in going into management—may no longer be the case.

A Long-term Coaching Scenario

Coaching for growth often deals with what is potentially there. But you may have to look for the potential. For example, here is an informal coaching session between Vincent and his boss, Kathryn.

Kathryn: Vincent, I have my own view of how you do your job, but I'd like to get a better idea of how you see your job. What do you like about it? What do you think you do best? Let's compare notes.

Vincent: What do I like best? Dealing with customers on the phone. I didn't used to like it. But I do now.

Kathryn: I got that impression. But you seem to be very good at it. What changed your mind?

Vincent: At first it was all so new. I really didn't know how to handle it. But I got to where I felt more confident about it.

Kathryn: Didn't the training session help?

Vincent: It was pretty general. There are a lot of things they didn't cover. You know, even if they did, you'd probably forget them. It's only after you've been on the phone for a while that you see all the things you have to know.

Kathryn: So you learned more by doing.

Vincent: Right.

Kathryn: Nancy told me you'd been a lot of help to her.

Vincent: She had some problems with some customers, and I showed her how I handled them.

Kathryn: She said you were quite good at showing her how to deal with some of the problems. You were very patient, I'm told.

Vincent: Well, I liked showing her. It was fun, especially since it worked.

Kathryn: Let's get back to the training. If the initial sessions aren't too helpful, do you think some follow-up sessions would be better?

Vincent: I think they would. Right now, we sit around over lunch and talk about the calls we get, and that helps sometimes. But I think an hour or so of follow-up training would be good once in a while.

Kathryn: How would we conduct that hour?

Vincent: One way would be to have everyone describe one kind of problem call, and then we'd talk about how to deal with it. Sort of go around the room and everyone contributes once. Then, when everyone has talked about one call, go around again. We could squeeze a lot into an hour.

Kathryn: Suppose we try it out. Would you like to run the session?

Vincent: Sure. That would be great!

Kathryn: Does that sort of thing —training—interest you?

Vincent: Yes. It's a great feeling to help someone else with a problem you've had.

Kathryn: Have you done much thinking about what you'd like to do after this? Or do you want to be a telephone representative indefinitely?

Vincent: I enjoy it. But I suppose I'll get a little tired of it. I haven't really thought much about it.

Kathryn: As I see it, if you do get tired and want to do something else, you've got a couple of choices. Have you thought about being a salesman? You're very good with customers.

Vincent: No, I don't see myself as a salesman.

Kathryn: But you already know a great deal about it. Would you be interested in training salespeople in customer service? Helping them to know what kinds of things customers ask for and how to respond?

Vincent: I think I'd like that very much. It gives me a lot of satis-faction learning how to work better, and then passing that along to others.

Kathryn: Maybe someday you'd like to do training full-time.

Vincent: I don't know, but I'd like to give your suggestions a try.

Kathryn: Okay. Let's start with the follow-up. We'll schedule an hour, and you let everyone know what's involved so they can think about their phone calls ahead of time. Then, you conduct the meeting. Is that all right?

Vincent: That's great!

Kathryn: If that goes well, and I'm sure it will, I'll talk with Marion Selby about your giving him a hand now and then with general sales training. You might do a session on customer service, as I said.

Vincent has already consented. For Kathryn, there is a short-term benefit. She will have better training for her customer service representatives. They will function better. She has found a talent in Vincent she and her employees can use.

Kathryn has suggested a step-by-step program of development to Vincent. The first will provide a test. If it works, and Vincent is still willing, they'll go to the next step. If that works, then it will probably be time for Vincent to think about the next step, which could be a full-time training position.

Coaching is a continuing process. Each session provides you with data you can use to plan future coaching. Eventually Kathryn may suggest to Vincent that he begin to acquire training skills, e.g., in giving oral presentations.

Specific situations can trigger coaching. For example:

Observed behavior. "That tenant

was irate when she walked in. Yet, you managed to calm her down and persuade her to pay up the rent she had been withholding. You are very good with people. You also seem to work well under pressure." Where might these skills lead?

The record. "You stepped in when Wayne was out because he broke his leg. Not only did you keep the operation going, you actually increased output by more than 20 percent by rearranging the work group." What does this accomplishment suggest?

Definable strengths. "Time after time, whenever there was an argument or a potential conflict in meetings, I've seen you step in and defuse the situation. Not only that, but people leave feeling good." How can this talent be put to general use?

Reports. "People I've talked to say they find you easy to work with. You're always coming up with suggestions that help lighten the work load." What is the significance of this asset?

However well-meaning your questions are, you have to consider the possibility that they may seem threatening to a subordinate, especially to one who is fairly new. There must be time for sufficient trust to be developed. Subordinates must be convinced that you really are concerned about their growth and development. They must be assured through your behavior that you won't ridicule them should they happen to discuss ambitions that are deep and hitherto unrevealed.

Once you uncover a potential skill, find out whether there is interest in developing it. You may have to spur the interest by describing the various situations in which a skill or a talent can be applied usefully. Is there sufficient interest to pursue it? If there is, what can be done to develop it? Should you suggest training? A program of education? Reading? Consultation with experts? An assignment?

Don't commit yourself to a course of action without first making sure that the employee is serious about it too.

In coaching, whether you start with general areas of strength, or with specific questions that are designed to elicit information on observed or reported behavior of accomplishments, try to end the session specifically. What is to be done? How it is to be done? In what time period?

One final caution: Do not come across as a psychologist. People tend to get nervous if they suspect you are defining them in psychological terms.

Adding What You Know

Coaching builds a sense of collaboration: We're both going for the same things; we can both get them if we work together. Collaboration requires openness between those involved in the working relationship. Thus a coaching session provides you with a chance to bring the employee up-to-date on changes that could affect his or her future. For example, you'll want to consider such potential obstacles or opportunities as:

Organizational changes. What departments or divisions are to be phased out or merged? What new managerial or professional functions are being contemplated?

Staffing changes. What internal expansions or cutbacks are being considered?

Budget changes. What money is being included for the first time or is being increased or reduced? In what areas? There might be a greater allowance, for instance, for management development or tuition refund.

New facilities. The construction of a plant, laboratory, or branch might offer significant opportunities for advancement, as would the acquisition of new companies.

New projects or plans. The launching of a new product, service, or program could open doors.

These are some of the significant developments in the offing that could be opportunities for career advancement. Even if, because of confidentiality, you can't be specific about the developments, you can at least give some advice as to how the employee can best prepare; what skills or knowledge would be helpful. One result of your coaching, you hope, will be that subordinates are encouraged to do their own assignments, to study the opportunities, to gauge their own talents in terms of the organization's needs, to develop a growth mentality that will discourage obsolescence.

But there can be another result of your extensive coaching, especially of key subordinates. Their coaching can be perceived as a reward for good performance and for the continuing actualization of potential skills. To the employee, you have taken the time to concern yourself with the employee's development because he or she is worth it.

Employee Preference Questionnaire

1. Please list those aspects, responsibilities, and duties of your job that you like most.

a. _____

b. _____

c. _____

d. _____

e. _____

f. _____

That you like least.

a. _____

b. _____

c. _____

d. _____

2. What functions or responsibilities of your job would you like to spend more time doing, if you could?

_____

_____

_____

_____

Spend less time doing, if you could?

_____

_____

_____

_____

3. If you had the opportunity, what kinds of work and responsibility that you are not now doing would you choose? _____

_____

_____

_____

_____

4. What skills, knowledge, and experience from training, education, previous employment or outside interests do you have that you believe would be useful in your current position or in different areas of responsibility that you would like to assume?

_____

_____

_____

_____

_____

_____

Employee Personal Data Form

Name of employee: _____

Date entered department: _____

Background Information

Education: _____

_____

_____

_____

_____

_____

Training prior to joining this department: _____

_____

_____

_____

_____

_____

Previous employment (beginning with most recent):

Dates: _____ Position: _____

  Principal responsibilities: _____

_____

Dates: _____ Position: _____

  Principal responsibilities: _____

_____

Dates: _____ Position: _____

  Principal responsibilities: _____

_____

Current Employment Information

Title or position held in this department (beginning with most recent):

Date: _____ Position/title: _____

  Principal responsibilities: _____

_____

_____

Dates: _____ Position/title _____

  Principal responsibilities: _____

_____

_____

Dates: _____ Position/title _____

  Principal responsibilities: _____

_____

_____

Training and education since employee entered the department or organization:

_____

_____

_____

_____

_____

Outside service, affiliations, avocations:

_____

_____

_____

_____

Outstanding professional/vocational accomplishments:

_____

_____

_____

_____

Skills Data

List those skills in which the employee has demonstrated exceptional competence:

_____

_____

_____

_____

_____

List those skills in which the employee has demonstrated acceptable or adequate competence:

_____

_____

_____

_____

List those skills or experiences that the employee's record suggests he or she has applied in previous employment or in which the employee has received training and education (but has not demonstrated in current employment):

_____

_____

_____

_____

List those skills or experiences that the employee may have gained in outside interests (see above) that might be useful in current or future positions:

_____

_____

_____

_____

Employee Development Data

What kinds of additional responsibilities/opportunities has the employee indicated an interest in?

_____

_____

_____

_____

What kinds of additional responsibilities/opportunities do your observation and records indicate that the employee might become qualified for?

_____

_____

_____

_____

List the additional responsibilities that you believe the employee is presently capable of assuming:

_____

_____

_____

_____

Long-term Coaching Interview Form

(You might wish to consult the Employee Personal Data form before conducting the interview. An example of such a form is found on page 119.)

Name of employee: _____

Title or position: _____

Length of time in title or position: _____

Date of previous coaching session: _____

1. What departmental responsibilities could the employee's abilities be applied to in the next twelve months?

_____

_____

_____

_____

_____

_____

2. Specify the principal work assignments the employee will undertake in the next six to twelve months.

a. _____

b. _____

c. _____

d. _____

e. _____

f. _____

3. What factors such as organizational and staff changes, budgeting, new facilities, project or plans might provide advantages or disadvantages for this employee?

_____

_____

_____

_____

_____

_____

4. What training, education, and experience has this employee had that is not now being applied substantially in his or her present responsibility?

_____

_____

_____

_____

_____

_____

5. What opportunities or considerations for the employee's growth and development lie in your answers to the preceding four questions?

_____

_____

_____

_____

_____

_____

6. What specific guidance or action plans are you offering the employee as a result of the information you have entered in Question 5?

a. _____

b. _____

c. _____

d. _____

e. _____

f. _____

7. What resources such as training, education, specific coaching by yourself or others are you recommending or making available to this employee?

_____

_____

_____

_____

_____

8. What other steps or reorganization will you undertake to help this employee to prepare more effectively for new responsibilities?

_____

_____

_____

_____

_____

9. Date for review of progress: _____

10. Date of next coaching session: _____

11. Your interim notes gleaned from observation, records, comments of others, etc., that update your knowledge of this employee and his or her potential growth areas:

_____

_____

_____

_____

_____

_____

_____

_____

_____

12. Preliminary notes that help you prepare for your next coaching session with this person:

_____

_____

_____

_____

_____

_____

_____

_____

_____

Managing Conflict

A healthy organization, one in which people are supportive and collaborative, is an almost inevitable by-product of people's efforts to find better ways to do things.

As a facilitator, you can help employees to work through their conflicts. It's more helpful to look for alternative ways to behave and to relate than to try to pin the blame on someone. You can help the disputants focus their energies on the positive rather than the negative. The people in conflict will also need your help in agreeing on the nature of the problem. People involved in disagreement often have varying perceptions of the disagreement. The following form can guide you as well as the disputants in your search for a solution to the conflict.

Each person involved in the dispute fills out the form.

Developing Alternatives to a Conflict Situation

I. Get the data. Each person in the dispute makes up four lists, as described below.

A. What I believe the other person should be doing:

_____

_____

_____

_____

_____

_____

_____

B. What he believes I should be doing:

_____

_____

_____

_____

_____

_____

_____

C. What I believe I should be doing:

_____

_____

_____

_____

_____

D. What he believes he should be doing:

_____

_____

_____

_____

_____

II. Edit the data. Review each of the preceding lists and change all negative statements to positive. Instead of suggesting that the other person stop doing something that you dislike, define an alternative behavior that you would find acceptable. For example, don't say, "He should stop writing memos to me." Rather, "He should communicate with me by telephone or face to face." When you finish, you should have four lists of positive statements.

III. Define common goals. Compare your lists and make a list of the common objectives you described in Step I.

_____

_____

_____

_____

_____

_____

_____

_____

IV. Make an action plan. For each of the mutually agreed upon objectives in Step 3, develop a detailed action plan describing the step, designating who is responsible for it, and when it must be accomplished.

Step: _____

_____

_____

_____

Responsibility: _____ Deadline: _____

Step: _____

_____

_____

_____

Responsibility: _____ Deadline: _____

Step: _____

_____

_____

_____

Responsibility: _____ Deadline: _____

Step: _____

_____

_____

_____

Responsibility: _____ Deadline: _____

Chapter Six

Giving Feedback

While employees are trying to perform according to your expectations and standards, they need feedback on how they are doing. It is probable that most employees receive far more negative feedback than positive. Getting much criticism and little praise can be a demoralizing and a demotivating experience.

Positive reinforcement, or feedback, can serve to let employees know they are doing well, can encourage repetition, and can reward.

Praise is a powerful reinforcer. Few employees will ever tell you that they receive very much of it, let alone an excess.

Praise is a reward that you have available to you all the time. It costs you nothing. It never really loses its effectiveness. And you never run out of it.

To evaluate your expertise in giving feedback, check yourself out on the following quiz.

Rating Yourself on Your Feedback Skills

To determine how effective you are at giving and receiving feedback, score yourself on the following scale:

4—always
3—more often than not
2—occasionally
1—rarely or never

1. I look for opportunities to tell employees how they are performing.   4   3   2   1

2. In my discussions with employees, I try to control the transaction (i.e., lead the discussion to my objective).   4   3   2   1

3. In discussions with me, I recognize that the employee has needs and wants that I should acknowledge.   4   3   2   1

4. In a serious discussion or an interview with an employee, I make sure I know what I want from it.   4   3   2   1

5. In such a discussion, I ask myself what I think the employee would like from the exchange.   4   3   2   1

6. During a meeting or discussion with others, I try to examine my own behavior frequently to determine whether I am effective (i.e., getting what I want from the transaction).   4   3   2   1

7. When I give feedback to subordinates, I work to influence their thinking and actions.   4   3   2   1

8. In the transactions that I initiate with employees, I consider myself a persuader to get the action I want from them.   4   3   2   1

9. When I give negative feedback to an employee, I am alert to the possibility that the other person will try to distract me from my objective.   4   3   2   1

10. In feedback situations, I work to involve employees in finding a solution to problems of performance.   4   3   2   1

11. I realize that, even as boss, I must, in communicating with employees, respect their opinions and explanations.   4   3   2   1

12. Even when criticizing an employee, I try to show that I respect him or her as a person though I disapprove of the person's actions.   4   3   2   1

13. When my feedback is negative, I accept the employee's opinion or belief in his or her explanation, without necessarily agreeing that it is justified.   4   3   2   1

14. However wrong I believe an employee's perceptions are in a negative feedback situation, I assume that the person takes them seriously.   4   3   2   1

15. I avoid responding to an employee's explanation of inadequate performance with a "yes, but" or another kind of discounting answer.   4   3   2   1

16. I respect the probability that an employee who is being criticized or counseled will probably have negative feelings about it.   4   3   2   1

17. I accept the employee's belief, when angry or embarrassed during my criticism, that he or she has a right to have those feelings.   4   3   2   1

18. I know the difference between accepting someone's emotions and agreeing that they are appropriate.   4   3   2   1

19. In feedback situations, I avoid talking about the employee's attitudes.	4	3	2	1
20. If a misunderstanding occurs during a feedback situation involving an employee, I take the blame for it.	4	3	2	1
21. I listen to employees in every feedback situation because I realize that every dialogue is different and represents an opportunity for me to learn something about the employee or about the department.	4	3	2	1
22. In discussions with employees, I believe that listening is usually just as important as talking.	4	3	2	1
23. When I listen, I practice making and maintaining eye contact.	4	3	2	1
24. When I listen to an employee, I make sure I don't interrupt.	4	3	2	1
25. In active listening, I try to sit back and look attentive without smiling or frowning.	4	3	2	1
26. When an employee is taking to me during a feedback situation, I try to analyze what the person is saying according to what I need to know, where the information leads me, and what connection it has with what I've already been told.	4	3	2	1
27. When an employee seems to find it difficult to talk in a criticism, appraisal, or counseling situation, I try to ask encouraging questions to get him or her to open up.	4	3	2	1
28. I make sure to limit distractions while an employee talks to me.	4	3	2	1
29. I frequently use pauses to emphasize my points when I give feedback to an employee.	4	3	2	1
30. When I give feedback, I make sure I am specific in telling the employee what performance I expect.	4	3	2	1
31. When I feel anger, I do not try to hide it, but let my expression and tone of voice reveal the fact.	4	3	2	1
32. When I encounter an employee's opposition to my counseling or criticism, I try to relax and listen before responding.	4	3	2	1
33. Before I respond to an employee's opposition during feedback, I first check with the employee to make sure I understand the person's meaning.	4	3	2	1
34. When an employee argues with or opposes my criticism or counseling, I interpret the opposition as a sign of involvement in the transaction.	4	3	2	1
35. When an employee shows anger with me, I remind myself that it may be a symptom of a greater problem than the one the person seems to be discussing with me at the time.	4	3	2	1

36. I let an angry employee get all the anger out before I try to deal with whatever has caused it.	4	3	2	1
37. When I start to give feedback to an employee, I know exactly what it is that I want the employee to do or to understand.	4	3	2	1
38. I believe it is important to know as much as I can about the employee before I start a feedback session.	4	3	2	1
39. I realize how important it is to involve the employee in the feedback session by asking questions to determine how much the other person is hearing of what I say.	4	3	2	1
40. I assume that it is my responsibility to spell out exactly what I want of the employee as a result of the feedback interview.	4	3	2	1
41. When an employee expresses opposition to my feedback, I consider the possibility that he or she doesn't clearly understand what I want.	4	3	2	1
42. I consciously use persuasive techniques when I give feedback rather than assuming that the employee will accept what I say simply because I am the boss.	4	3	2	1
43. I believe in being positive in a feedback interview and assume that the employee also wants something good to result from the session.	4	3	2	1
44. I subscribe to the belief that when I convey the conviction that performance ought to be at a certain level, I increase the probability that I will get the performance I want.	4	3	2	1
45. I really believe that most employees want to increase their effectiveness on the job and will welcome my guidance, even if it is critical.	4	3	2	1

Scoring Your Feedback Skills Inventory

If your score is more than *150*, you already know that you are highly effective in your feedback interviews. No doubt there are a few holes to plug, and your lower scores on individual questions will show you where. Other than that, you have some fine-tuning to do overall.

If your score is more than *120* but less than *151*, you are generally effective but may be occasionally dis-appointed that you do not achieve your objectives as completely as you'd like. Review the quiz to better understand why.

If your score lies between *90* and *121*, chances are good that you enter feedback sessions without the confidence of success that you'd like and complete them feeling disappointed or ambivalent about your effectiveness.

Finally, if you score below *90*, you need a serious review of the feedback and communications techniques in this section.

Saying "Thank You" and "Keep It Up"

If you are to be successful in upgrading the performance and skills of your employees, you must keep this in mind at all times: Reward the behavior you want; don't reward the behavior you don't want. The employees' behavior that you reward is very likely to be the behavior they repeat. If you concentrate on rewarding actual achievement rather than friendliness, loyalty, and general goodwill, that will be where you enjoy your return on your investment.

Make sure that employees recognize what it is that you are rewarding. Don't rely on the annual merit increases to convey your thanks. Probably everyone gets them. When everyone is rewarded the same way, no one is. Don't treat everyone equally. People who do a better job for you should get the better and more frequent rewards.

But it is not only what reward you give, but *how* you give it that will encourage repeated desired behavior. The following rules will help you praise effectively. They also apply to any reward you can give:

1. Be consistent. When praiseworthy performance occurs, don't miss the chance to praise it. When people have made a change, have been successful with the work you assigned, have taken responsibility for applying their training or following your coaching, let them know how pleased you are and how successful they have been. Soon people will understand—because you are consistent—that you want good work and will recognize it. You don't have to tell good performers every day that they are good. You **do** have to remember to reinforce them intermittently. And when someone really

excels on a task or assignment, don't be inhibited. Furthermore, whenever an employee successfully applies new skills or knowledge, give praise. How often you praise or otherwise reward depends on how much the employee achieves and how consistent the employee is in achieving it.

2. Be specific. Managers sometimes say such things as, "You're doing a great job" or "Keep up the good work." Such comments may be better than no recognition, but they don't have much impact. The trouble is that they don't define what aspects of an employee's performance you like. For example, one of your employees is very good with customers on the phone. You say, "Mary, what's admirable about your telephone manner is that you never let a customer rattle you, no matter how angry he gets. You always concentrate on solving the problem. You've probably saved us a lot of customers."

A subordinate writes clear, concise reports. You can say, "I appreciate how you make your points clearly and quickly. I never have to read several pages to find out what the report is all about. I wish everyone could write as well as you. It would make my job a lot easier."

The more specific you are about what you like and want, the greater the likelihood that it will be repeated; the subordinate will feel complimented that you were so observant. Finally, your specificity prevents you from falling into the sameness trap. Your feedback doesn't always sound alike.

3. Praise soon after the performance. What the employee has done is still fresh in his or her mind shortly after the activity or the event. Recognizing the performance immediately offers a better chance that the desired behavior will be repeated.

Also, immediacy underlines the value you put on the specific performance. "Susan, I appreciate the way you filled in for Abby this morning. I thought we were in for it when she got sick and had to go home, especially since the Wright proposal had to go out. But you stepped in, organized things, got the proposal done. And without a moan or a groan. That's something I value so much about you."

Delayed recognition of praiseworthy performance sometimes conveys a by-the-way quality. The praise loses impact. There is the unfortunate suggestion that the behavior wasn't worth mentioning.

How effective are you in giving rewards and recognizing good performance? Here's an exercise that will help you judge:

a. Make a list of your subordinates. After each name, list the person's performance characteristics that contribute to getting the work done for the accomplishment of your objectives.
b. Ask yourself these questions: How recently have I recognized that performance? How regularly have I rewarded the behavior I want?
c. Review the checklist of rewards on page 75. Of how many have you availed yourself?

What you will probably find is that you are not regularly and predictably recognizing the good work that people do. Furthermore, don't be surprised if you discover that you are reinforcing with only a fraction of the rewards available to you.

Keep in mind that increasing the value of the work requires continual effort. But the payoff in productivity is worth it.

Giving Criticism Ineffectively

Giving criticism—there is probably no other managerial task that tests your skills and resolve in quite the way that giving negative feedback does. But the need is clear. One of your salespeople is careless about filling out order forms and, as a result, unhappy customers receive wrong or incomplete shipments. A secretary comes to work late repeatedly, and she disappears from her desk for long periods of time during the day. Your senior analyst turns in a report that contains errors serious enough to invalidate certain conclusions and to make some projections suspect. A supervisor botches the handling of a disciplinary problem through not following recommended procedures.

All four situations call for criticism. You cannot permit the continuation of such performance. It violates your standards. If you neglect taking corrective procedures, you are simply throwing away a potential resource—the employee who could be performing effectively. Any tolerance of bad work on your part will have repercussions among other employees, either in lowered morale, lessened motivation, or a decline in respect for you.

The erring employee won't seek your criticism but will usually accept it, even welcome it. Few employees want to be seen by others as bumbling, lazy, careless, or indifferent. Few people can tolerate such a perception of themselves. If your criticism is designed to help inadequate performers to become more effective, they will. And in time, they will thank you for it.

But there is pain in criticism, for you, as well as for the employee. Chances are both of you are embarrassed to be going through such a process. It's almost an understatement to suggest that giving negative feedback is not one of managers' favorite tasks. To soften the hurt for both people, some managers will resort to techniques that are unsound. Other managers, perhaps believing that most employees will resist criticism, choose approaches that are guaranteed to arouse resentment and anger in the person being criticized. All such techniques are self-defeating for the manager, because they seriously erode the manager's base of respect and credibility. Subsequent criticism sessions with employees who have been "protected" or pressured will be even less effective.

For example, here are four feedback techniques that many managers use although they should be avoided: **the sandwich, sandbagging, the broadside, and psychoanalysis.**

The sandwich technique involves placing a slab of criticism between two slices of praise. In the case of the senior analyst who has generally performed well but has begun to be careless, a manager might be tempted to use the sandwich, and here's how it would work:

"Court, come in and sit down. I've been wanting to talk with you for some time, but you know how it is. The squeaky wheel and all that. I guess that's the contradiction. The people who are causing all the problems get my time, and someone like you who works hard and does well gets very little attention. You've generally been reliable and conscientious, although I guess everyone has an off day now and then. Like the report you turned in last Tuesday. I don't know whether you're aware of the mistakes, but they had to do an extensive reworking of it upstairs. I'm passing it along to you because some of the folks up there were pretty unhappy. I told them that it is unusual for you to be that far off. But I think it's best to mention it to you. And I know that with you, a word is sufficient. I don't have many people in the department who are as concerned as you are about the quality of your work. Well, I'm glad we were able to have this chat after such a long time."

If Courtney walks away from the boss a bit puzzled about what has happened to him, he's justified. In mixing praise with criticism, this manager risks diluting the impact of both. The negative part of the feedback seems almost incidental, with a definite by-the-way quality. The praise has been contaminated by the criticism. The more poor Court thinks about the "chat," the more upset he will get. He has been manipulated, although the manager would plead that his only concern was to soften the impact of the criticism so that it wouldn't devastate an otherwise good employee. But the manager was trying to avoid the pain as well.

The next time the analyst hears his boss praise him, he'll be so busy wondering when the other shoe will drop that he won't hear or appreciate the good things the boss is saying about him.

Sandbagging can be cruel. It gets its name from a trick used in poker, when one person checks another into a cinch. A player who feels strongly that he has a winning hand does not bet but rather checks, that is, passes without betting. His aim is to lure another player into making a bet so that the checker can raise heavily. Most poker players frown on the practice.

The following example demonstrates how a manager will check a subordinate into a cinch. The salesman's boss is talking to him about a problem caused by careless order-taking.

Manager: The Apwell people say their shipment was all fouled-up.
Subordinate: I know, but I got it all straightened out. I've had a lot of trouble with those people. They can't make buying decisions. They say one thing today, another tomorrow. They're always changing the order after it's submitted. Anyway, I got it all straightened out. Don't worry about it.
Manager: As far as you know, they're happy.
Subordinate: That's what they tell me.
Manager: Well, that's not what they tell me. I got this letter from them this morning, listing about five or six occasions in the last few months when you've ignored their instructions and fouled things up. They're not happy. In fact, they tell me that if it happens one more time, they're going elsewhere. What do you say about that?"

The salesman has been trapped. He won't forget this interview with his boss. And very likely what he will remember is not that he didn't tell the truth or that he hadn't done his job, but that his boss sandbagged him. And he'll resent it.

It's one thing to hold the winning cards. It's quite another to play them in such a way that another is humiliated.

Firing a *broadside* often results in spreading a problem rather than containing it. One Los Angeles executive's office overlooked the parking lot for his company, and he grew tired of seeing so many empty spaces after eight o'clock, when employees were supposed to be at work. So he wrote a memo for company-wide circulation to remind employees that they were expected to arrive on time and not, as he had observed, at twenty or thirty minutes after start-up time.

Such a broadside memo condemns the innocent along with the guilty. The innocent are offended because their conscientious arrival has not been recognized. The guilty conclude that everyone else has been doing the same thing they have. Why stop?

Sometimes a general criticism will make management a target for employee ridicule. One company issued a memo reminding all employees that it was against policy for employees to show up at work under the influence of alcohol or to use drugs on the company premises. There was no explanation behind issuing the memo. It arrived out of the blue. Many employees reacted by laughing and asking, "Who's been having all the fun?" Probably no constructive result was achieved.

If the broadside approach is ineffective, why do managers resort to it? One explanation is that they don't want to confront a single offender or a small group of offenders. Again, the pain and embarrassment of giving feedback face to face may be more than the managers want to suffer. So they do it by paper. There is another reason why they may resort to shotgun criticism: laziness. It takes work to identify the guilty parties, so the paper route seems easier.

Before committing criticism to paper, the manager should ask these questions:

- Do I really have a sound, defensible reason for expressing this criticism on paper?

- Am I hiding behind paper because I shrink from a personal confrontation?
- Is every person to whom it is directed guilty?
- Will the memo actually achieve the desired change of behavior or merely create hostility?
- Is there a better way than the written word? For example, group discussions?

Conducting a *psychoanalysis* is the fourth approach to criticism that can backfire and cause lasting harm. In this approach, the manager not only tells the erring employee what he or she has done but **why** it was done, what psychological motivation was behind it. Following is a scenario in which the manager uses the psychoanalytic technique to give negative feedback to a subordinate:

Manager: Because you didn't follow the proper procedures, we now have an employee who is threatening us with a discrimination action. How did you slip up?
Subordinate: I got so worked up about what he did that I forgot.
Manager: So you do acknowledge that you knew what you were supposed to do.
Subordinate: I guess so.
Manager: You guess so, but you still didn't do it.
Subordinate: I told you. I forgot.
Manager: I have to wonder about that. I can think of other times when I thought you were reluctant to follow instructions. I don't think it's an accident. You really ought to ask yourself whether you have a problem accepting authority. That's a pretty serious thing for a supervisor, not being able to accept authority.
Subordinate: I don't know that I have a problem.

Manager: Well, maybe you'd better think about that.

This exchange could go on forever, with inconsequential results. The question has shifted from what the employee did wrong to whether he has an authority problem. Anytime the manager leaves the subject of behavior and talks about psychological motivation or attitude, neither of which can be seen or measured, he or she is entering a morass.

The preceding four techniques—sandwiching, sandbagging, firing a broadside, playing psychoanalyst—may seem to lessen the pain of criticizing or to reduce the chance of opposition in the person criticized, but in the long run, they'll cause even greater problems. Furthermore, some of the benefits of constructive criticism (in addition to immediate correction of deficient behavior)—learning and measurement of performance—are lost or made more difficult to achieve.

Criticism That Works

If your objective is to have an effective, motivated work group, then you must be prepared to give negative feedback, however painful. Your subordinates must know when they are doing well, and when they are not. And when they are not, they must know how to improve their performance. Forget about the pain and embarrassment. There's little you can do about them. Concentrate instead on creating the proper conditions for enabling the subordinate to understand and accept what you have to say. You might wish to follow these steps in criticizing:

1. Describe the behavior you want corrected or eliminated. Stick to behavior. As you've already read, don't get trapped into talking about attitudes. You may be tempted to say to your secretary who comes in late, "You have a poor work attitude." But that is your opinion. You can't back it up with factual data. You can't measure an attitude. And the employee may argue with you or protest that you are being unfair (there might be extenuating circumstances). When you point out, however, that the employee has been more than fifteen minutes late to work three mornings this week, and that others had to answer more than twenty calls in her absence from the department, you are being clear and indisputable.

The behavior you describe should be that which you have observed. You don't want to be passing on hearsay. That opens the door to a lot of argument. The exception to this rule is when you discuss behavior that has been documented by the employee's immediate supervisor.

2. Criticize as soon as possible after seeing the behavior. The ideal time is immediately after the event. The closer you are in time, the more precise you can be, since it's fresh in your mind. It's also clear in the employee's mind. Immediacy and specificity tend to preclude argument. "You told the customer that if she didn't like the store policy, it was too bad. There are better and more courteous ways of saying that." The subordinate may have explanations for why she said it that way, but if it happened a minute ago, she can hardly deny that she did it.

There's another good reason for catching the mistake quickly: It won't be repeated. Or at least you diminish that possibility. A third reason for acting right away is that you head off a buildup of tension in the employee. If he or she is aware that the performance wasn't what it

should have been, and knows that you know it, then the subordinate will have some anxious feelings until you resolve the matter.

3. Get the employee's agreement that what was done was not in accordance with your standards. Of course, taking this step presumes that you have been clear about what standards of performance you expect. Don't go any further in the criticism process until you are sure that the employee understands what you find objectionable. Nothing takes your wind away faster than to have an employee hear you out, then say, "I don't see what you're making such a fuss about." Does she understand that by being away from her desk for long, unexplained periods of time that she is forcing others to do her work for her? That others resent the fact and you disapprove?

If you've been clear about your standards, and others have accepted them without complaint, you don't need to get into a debate as to whether they're reasonable and right. All you need to do at this stage of the process is to get the other's agreement that his or her performance deviates from the desired.

4. Make sure you hear the employee's analysis of the situation. Whatever you have observed, consider that the employee may have seen the situation differently. The employee may have missed an important deadline, but she tells you there was another person or a procedure that at least contributed to the delay. You can expect an employee who feels on the spot to be defensive, maybe even antagonistic. But it helps to let the employee sound off a bit, make explanations, even rationalize, if you are to win acceptance of your recommendations for improvement. It's possible that you will learn something about your department that you don't know, such as that there is another person who interferes with your assignments or a supervisor who gives conflicting instructions. Also, you may find that the employee doesn't know what to do or how to do it, doesn't understand the seriousness of doing the job right, or believes that his or her methods are better than yours. You then have some reorienting or training to do.

However, don't let yourself be sidetracked by lengthy excuses or explanations. The secretary may tell you that her baby-sitter is frequently late, and that she has car trouble and hasn't been able to get the car fixed, etc. If you feel you're in danger of losing control of the interview, go on to the next step.

5. Emphasize that you want and expect improvement. Once you have an understanding and agreement that there is a gap between what is and what should be, get the employee's help in looking for solutions. Use the assertive-responsive approach. The employee probably doesn't feel good about not doing the job well. He or she certainly has some resources to bring to the search for a solution or improvement.

If the employee seems absorbed in explanations and rationalizations long after you've ceased to find them useful to the interview, continue to emphasize the point of it all: improvement. "Yes, I understand that your car needs work, that it keeps breaking down, but I want you here on time, every morning. How do we accomplish that?"

Agree on what is to be done, by whom, how, and in what time frame. You may want to ask the employee to restate what the two of you have agreed on just to be sure that the employee has heard what you meant to be heard. Let your subordinate know

that this agreement is a "contract" that you expect him or her to fulfill. Also, be sure that the employee knows there will be a follow-up session if the solution is not applied or does not work. The important message to give at this time is "I know you want to do a good job, and I want to help you to do it. That's why we've had this talk."

By emphasizing future effectiveness, alternative behaviors, and solutions, you're not precluded from defining causes of the problem performance. In fact, it may be necessary to eliminate certain causes and contributing factors before a solution can be made to work. But, often, a search for causes can be translated into blame and fault-finding. Thus, unless it is absolutely necessary to dig into the past, concentrate on the future and its improvement, not the history of the deficiency (except in the case of a continuing deficiency that the employee has not corrected). Again, the assertive-responsive mode works just fine: "I'm not happy about this situation. I don't think you're happy either. What change can we bring about that will make both of us feel better?"

Mixing Positive with Negative Feedback

Some managers like to say nice things along with the negative things. To be specific, they like to open the criticism session with some complimentary remarks. For example, managers point out what the employee has done well, or how long the employee has been around, giving fine service, etc. If a manager pursues such a practice, employees will begin to hear, "On the one hand," or, "On the positive side of the ledger," even though the manager never utters such phrases. Ironically, managers who preface criticism with praise say they do so to relax the employee and make him or her more receptive to the negative feedback. As you can imagine, the opposite occurs, once the employee is onto the formula. Chances are that the employee does not really hear the praise. He or she is too busy wondering what is about to be unloaded. So, the praise is probably wasted, but worse, the employee begins to view the manager as a manipulator, as someone not to be totally trusted.

Yet, there are times when good and bad must be delivered together. Perhaps there is a need for the employee to get a total picture of whatever the person is involved in. Or it is time for a progress report. Or maybe you don't get to see the employee very often, and you must take advantage of the occasion.

If you believe that the message must be a mixed one, guard against the dilution and contamination that you saw as a danger in the sandwich technique described earlier. The following recommendations can help you to convey both positive and negative feedback without doing great harm to the impact of either:

1. Start with the negative. Get it out of the way. You don't want it to spoil the good feedback later. Announce that you're going to start with the criticism. You might say, "I have some positive feedback for you later, but let's get the criticism out of the way." Cover what is wrong without mixing in any praise. The subordinate can concentrate on your praise without having to worry about what might follow.

2. Get agreement on the points of your criticism before leaving it. Understandably, you may be tempted to get through the minuses as quickly as possible to get to the more

pleasant pluses. But there's no profit in throwing away the criticism, which will happen if the person on the receiving end doesn't agree. You must have agreement before you can be confident that corrective action will, in fact, be taken.

3. Agree on remedial action if required. What will be the solution or alternative required? Agreement is one thing; a firm action plan is another.

4. Keep positives and negatives in proportion. Once you've caused pain, you may want to exaggerate some of the good features of the subordinate's work. But that won't be helpful if your exaggeration of the pluses tends to diminish the importance of the minuses. So keep the two messages in proportion to each other. If the major part of the feedback is critical, then you might want to say, "There are some good things I want to say about your work. They're encouraging, although not as substantial in their content as the negative points. The most important things for you to take away from this discussion are the action plans to correct the problems."

If the positives far outweigh the negatives, you might say, "I have to cover some areas of criticism. There aren't many, but they are important. Once we have taken care of them, I want to get on with the more pleasant aspects."

5. Don't return to a discussion of the negative. You have already established an understanding of what is wrong and what should be done about it. Leave it. You don't want to take the pleasure out of the praise.

Benefiting from the Criticism

Criticism is obviously a learning experience for the person receiving the feedback. But it should be for you as well. If you do not see the criticism session as a chance for you to learn, you could miss much. For example, you could lose the opportunity to uncover some organizational problems you didn't know existed; problems that interfere with motivation of subordinates. It's true that you don't want to be sidetracked during a criticism interview with an employee's baseless charges of this or that, but it is equally true that you don't want to ignore related problems that cry out for attention. The criticized employee might not have been able to meet the deadline because of a conflict that has developed between two supervisors whose cooperation she needed.

You might even discover that you are part of the problem. The employee may say, "Yes, I agree the job was not done right. But every time I made some progress, you interrupted me to have me help out on something else."

Criticism is an investment in individual employees and the work group you are building. If the work is to be done as you want it to be done,

---

Do's and Don'ts of Criticizing

DO be private with your criticism. Your primary objective is to gain a change of behavior, not to humiliate the subordinate, not to reduce his or her standing with co-workers. It's unlikely that the employee will hear much of what you are saying if he or she is concerned about what others think.

DON'T punish the employee. Punishment in this context is not the same as discipline. If there are prescribed disciplinary measures you must take as a result of the employee's action, do so. But don't otherwise inflict punishment. Some managers will be sarcastic, use demeaning language, drag out a laundry list of past or minor offenses, all designed to grind the employee down. You don't want the employee to become so angry or to feel like a hopeless case so that change in behavior is remote.

DO be patient. Many criticism sessions are usually over quickly. After all, neither of you wants to prolong the agony. But if the employee shows that he or she needs more time than usual, to understand, to accept, to discuss—be prepared to take that time. When you do, the employee will no doubt view your willingness to hear him or her out as an indication of your respect. In general, it's a good idea not to undertake criticism when you are rushed.

DON'T be personal. You are questioning an aspect of the employee's behavior, not the person's value or worth. Do not discuss personality; do not guess at attitudes; do not talk about characteristics except as they are manifested by behavior. For example, don't suggest that an employee has a "stubborn streak." Instead, point out that on several occasions the employee has not followed instructions.

DO be positive and hopeful. Convey the message that you know the employee wants to work more effectively. Be considerate and courteous even though firm; look for solutions rather than lay blame. After the criticism session, try to have some contact, no matter how brief, with the chastised employee that is of a normal operational nature. That way the employee will realize that the criticism has not ruptured your working relationship.

you have to insist that behavior that gets in the way be corrected—and the sooner, the better.

Criticism is really a considerate act. The employee wants to do the work as it should be done. Others in the work group have an interest in the employee's doing the job well. Your feedback, even though it is negative, is necessary and welcome because it guides the employee to better results.

Checking Yourself on Your Criticizing Skills

Here are examples of a criticism session. Analyze each and compare your analyses with those that immediately follow each example.

Example A

Manager: Charlie, if I have told you once, I've told you a dozen times, when you pick up a carton, don't lean over. Bend from your knees as you lift. When I tell you these things, I'm not just yakking because I like to hear myself talk.
Subordinate: Look, Ralph, don't get your blood pressure up. I just forgot.
Manager: That's what you always say. Are you getting prematurely senile?
Subordinate: What is the big fuss? I lift a carton, big deal.
Manager: The big deal is that one of these days you're not going to be able to straighten, and you'll be out on a workers' compensation claim for a back injury incurred on the job. And I'll tell you something right now. I'm going to fight that claim. You're not going to lie around the house collecting your pay, not when you've ignored me so many times.

Analysis of Example A

The manager is specific about describing the objectionable behavior. He reminds the employee that he has spoken about the faulty lifting method before, although the manager suggests that something is wrong with the employee's mind, that the subordinate keeps forgetting. A bit later, the manager implies that the forgetting is on purpose when he uses the word "ignored." The subordinate will no doubt resist the implication that he is being willful in not using the recommended technique. It's so easy to avoid the resistance that is rooted in an employee's feeling accused and demeaned. The manager appears angry, and no doubt he has justification for his anger. He should acknowledge that he is "hot under the collar," but should scrupulously avoid punitive, humiliating language.

Equally serious is the employee's seeming failure to understand why the manager makes a "big deal" of the incident. Early on, the manager could have worked to circumvent such resistance by having the employee agree that the manager had called the faulty method to his attention before. The employee would have to acknowledge that failure to act on the previous feedback by itself constituted problem behavior. Then the manager could have followed up the agreement by reminding the employee why it was policy to lift using the knees—to avoid injury and, possibly, a disputed claim.

This manager faces the possibility that the objectionable behavior will be repeated.

Example B

Manager: Come on in, Chuck. How are you?

Subordinate: Pretty good.

Manager: And the family?

Subordinate: Except for a case of chicken pox, they're fine.

Manager: You're very close to your family, aren't you?

Subordinate: I try to be.

Manager: There is such a thing as being too close, you know.

Subordinate: What do you mean?

Manager: Well, I would have thought by reading your call reports that you were spending quite a bit of time home instead of out selling. You've been averaging only about twelve calls per week. I thought you and I agreed you'd average sixteen to eighteen.

Analysis of Example B

You're right if you pegged this manager's approach as sandbagging. From the outset, the small talk seemed designed to put the salesman at ease. Probably the family issue was introduced with a smile. Quite appropriate for a casual conversation, terribly inappropriate for a criticism session.

A more constructive approach would have incorporated the following stages:

1. The manager's announcement that he had been reading Chuck's call reports and was disturbed to find that the weekly average of sales calls was down seriously.

2. An agreement with Chuck that in their last goal-setting session the number of sales calls to be made each week would average sixteen to eighteen.

3. A chance for Chuck to explain the disparity between objective and performance.

Even if the manager had not sandbagged, he would be better advised to skip the small talk in the begin-ning. It establishes the wrong atmosphere for a serious talk.

Example C

Manager: Sheila, come in, please, and close the door.

Subordinate: You wanted to see me?

Manager: Yes, sit down. I want to do some straight talking with you. I'm very unhappy with certain aspects of your performance. And I think you have too much potential to throw away your future here. I truly believe that. If I didn't, I wouldn't bother. I'd just give you a warning, and that's all.

Subordinate: A warning about what?

Manager: Being away from your desk for long periods of time. No one is quite sure where you go. But the other people in your department are complaining about having to cover for you, answer the telephone, look up files that are needed right away. So, yesterday I made a point of looking in on you from time to time. I couldn't stand at your desk all day, but I did notice that three out of four times I walked by, you were gone. One time, you'll recall, I left a message on your desk to call me as soon as you got back. It was close to a half hour before you called.

Subordinate: I wasn't feeling well.

Manager: I have to level with you. I had the rest room checked a couple of times by another woman. You weren't there. Where did you go?

Subordinate: Outside the building.

Manager: Remember I said there have been complaints about

other days? Apparently, some of your associates have kept a log. Here it is. Take a look at it and tell me whether you agree with it.

Subordinate: Did Marcy do this?

Manager: What difference does it make?

Subordinate: Because she's been on my case since Day One. She's a troublemaker.

Manager: Funny. No one else has said that about her.

Subordinate: This is just the kind of thing she'd do. I don't think this is accurate. Why did she do this?

Manager: I'm not saying that Marcy did this. In fact, I think it was a joint effort. The reason they gave it to me is that they say they don't want to have to do their work load and yours too.

Subordinate: I think it's unfair for you to use this thing against me. You can't know whether it's even close to the truth. You take their word over mine.

Manager: As a matter of fact, I don't. I saw your absences yesterday. I'm told there have been others days like it. I'm asking you whether that's correct.

Subordinate: I can't stand working around some of them. Like Marcy. I just have to get away. They're rude. I can't have a decent conversation with them. I have to get away. There's a friend of mine over in processing, and sometimes I talk to her.

Analysis of Example C

Notice what can happen when a manager introduces hearsay into the criticism session. Suddenly, it's a question of whose word should he take. He was correct in making his own observations as a result of hearing the complaints, and he should have stuck with what he saw.

Some people would feel that this manager started off using the sandwich approach with his statement, "I think you have too much potential to throw away your future here. . . ." He went on to say that his treatment of her would be quite different if he didn't believe that. Why bother to make a statement that could cloud the issue? The point is, certain aspects of her performance are objectionable. They need to be corrected regardless of whether she is considered to be high potential or not. Such a statement is beside the point. It may be harmless. It may, however, embolden the subordinate to resist your criticism. Therefore, it's best to avoid such comments.

The introduction of the log opened the door to distracting issues. One was the question of who did it? Was it Marcy? If so, Sheila termed her a "troublemaker." The manager immediately colludes in the sidetracking by saying he'd never heard that about Marcy. The issue was quite irrelevant. The issue of the log's accuracy would appear to be relevant, but it would have been better had the manager kept the log to himself.

In short, the criticism session concerns itself too much with the past and with behavior that might or might not have taken place.

The manager would have been on surer ground had he conducted the interview along the following lines:

"You were absent from your desk for long periods of time yesterday. Other people complained that they had to do your work as well as theirs. Would you like to comment on those unexplained absences?"

The manager takes time to hear Sheila out.

"I want you to know that when you simply disappear without any of us knowing why or where, you place a burden on others who have to cover for you. I can understand you're going to the rest room or to take a drink of water. I'm not nit-picking. But once yesterday I left a note asking you to call me when you returned, and it was a half hour before you did. That kind of absence I don't want. Do you understand why?"

Sheila agrees that the boss has a right to object.

"Then I want you to promise me that if you have to be away for any period of time, other than to take the breaks that I referred to, you should let me know. If you don't, and I see that you've disappeared as you did yesterday, I'll consider that a breach of our agreement."

The manager has Sheila's agreement, has remained fixed on future acceptable behavior, and has avoided all the sidetracking that went on in the sample.

Record of Criticism Interview

(In the case of repeated or continuing deficient or objectional behavior, you may, for purposes of documentation, wish to keep the following record on file.)

Name of employee: _____

Department/position: _____

Problem or event: _____

_____

_____

Date observed: _____ Date of interview: _____

Date of previous interview, same subject: _____

Change agreed to: _____

_____

_____

_____

Anticipated results of change: _____

_____

_____

_____

Resources (if necessary) to be supplied: _____

_____

_____

Date for change to be accomplished: _____

Type of follow-up or monitoring: _____

_____

_____

Further action, if necessary: _____

_____

_____

Checklist for a Criticism Interview

1. I criticized as soon as possible after the event or behavior.   _____
2. The interview was in private.   _____
3. I stuck to describing the deficient or objectional behavior.   _____
4. I described the behavior specifically.   _____
5. The behavior I discussed was observed by me (except for a
supervisor's documented report).   _____
6. I avoided discussing attitudes.   _____
7. I avoided discussing previous, unrelated behaviors that
were also a problem.   _____
8. I avoided interviewing while angry (or at least I acknowl-
edged my anger at the outset).   _____
9. I did not repeat hearsay.   _____
10. I did not mix positive with negative feedback.   _____
11. I took time to make sure that the employee understood
and agreed on the problem.   _____
12. I listened carefully to the employee's analysis of the
problem.   _____
13. When discussion strayed, I reminded the employee of the
change desired.   _____
14. I enlisted the employee's aid in looking for an alternative
or solution.   _____
15. If the problem was beyond the control of the employee, I
made a note to develop an action plan for improving condi-
tions.   _____
16. I emphasized the consequences of continuing the unde-
sired behavior.   _____
17. I accepted the employee's feelings.   _____

18. The employee and I agreed on an action plan for improvement. ⎯⎯⎯⎯

19. I made sure that the employee understood what was to be done. ⎯⎯⎯⎯

20. We agreed on a time frame for accomplishment of the change and what follow-up would be done. ⎯⎯⎯⎯

21. I looked for something I could learn from the discussion. ⎯⎯⎯⎯

22. In the case of objectional or deficient behavior that was repeated or continued, I made a record for my file that would constitute documentation for the future. ⎯⎯⎯⎯

Chapter Seven

Counseling

Counseling is a serious effort on your part to help an employee become or return to being an effective contributor in your work group. An employee who is not performing up to your standards, who has been evaluated as such, and criticized for those performance shortcomings, is a candidate for counseling. There was a time when managers tended to wash their hands of continually poor performing employees. When they became sufficiently tired or fed up with the deficient performances, the managers simply fired those employees and replaced them.

Today, there are certain constraints on managers in dealing with poor performance. First, there is the ethical consideration. Has the manager done everything reasonable in his or her power to help the employee to be effective? In the past, many managers didn't assume responsibility for employees' performance. People worked or they didn't

work. No one is that simplistic these days. You have to satisfy yourself that you haven't shortchanged the employee in any way, thereby possibly contributing to the deficiency. Counseling is your way of taking that final step to help the employee do what you want, what you hope he or she is capable of doing.

A second constraint in dealing with a deficient performer is economic. Presumably, the poor performer has been around for a time, long enough to know something of the operation. If you can help him or her remove the barrier that keeps the employee from being effective, then you have an employee who doesn't need training or a breaking-in period. It becomes more cost-effective to rescue a deficient performer than to go outside and bring in a stranger.

The laws provide a third constraint. Gone is the time when you could call the low performer into your office and say, "You're fired." If you don't have sufficient documentation showing that the employee was warned and given a reasonable chance to turn his or her performance around, you may find yourself facing an expensive action. Counseling helps you with such documentation.

For the manager, there are at least two givens in counseling a deficient performer. First, the process requires certain skills, and these skills will be described later on. Second, the interview causes stress, for both you and the employee. You should accept that. Don't deny it. It's very normal. No one likes to confront another person with that person's failure.

Following the recommendations in this section will help you to reduce that stress.

Preparing for the Interview

Assemble your evidence, your documentation. When did you speak with the employee about the deficiency? What performance improvements were agreed to—and not fulfilled? A copy of the performance evaluation in which the deficiency was noted should be part of your file. If you have a goal-setting program, have available the agreements that the employee could not achieve.

Pre-Counseling Checklist

The following checklist can sometimes help you in analyzing performance problems prior to counseling. From your observation and knowledge of the individual, and from the history of your relationship with the subordinate, you may be able to arrive at the appropriate recommendations for performance improvement without going through the counseling process.
Employees who fail seriously:

- ☐ Don't know what they're supposed to do.
- ☐ Don't know how to do it.
- ☐ Don't know why they should perform a particular job, task, or assignment.
- ☐ Face obstacles beyond their control.
- ☐ Don't think that what they've been instructed to do will work.
- ☐ Think their way of doing it is better.

- ☐ Are not achieving their personal objectives in the type of work assigned or in their working environment.
- ☐ Don't have the required abilities.
- ☐ Are personally and temperamentally unsuited to the work.
- ☐ Don't have sufficient time to do it.
- ☐ Are working on wrong priority items.
- ☐ Think they are performing well, in the absence of feedback.
- ☐ Are receiving poor supervision.
- ☐ Have personal problems that are distracting them or interfering in some way with work performance.

If you are not sure about any of these contributing factors, counseling is indicated. Even if you are, you may wish to proceed with the counseling process to enlist the employee's aid in solving the problem or for documentation purposes.

Objective evidence is necessary if you are to avoid the interminable arguing of the Yes-you-did-No-I-didn't (or the other way around).

Concentrate on the most important deficiency, if there is more than one. Don't bring in a laundry list of problem areas. You want to help the employee, not devastate him or her. Some managers are led into making such a list because they fear that the employee will not accept the evidence unless it is overwhelming. People can't change themselves simultaneously on a broad front. Improvement is usually focused and in increments.

Be clear about what kind of performance you want—indeed, insist upon—as a consequence of the counseling. You'll need that clarity in developing an action plan for improvement. Also, assume that the employee wants to be effective. It's a rare person who doesn't mind failing or being seen as a bumbler. The psychological evidence is all too convincing that people regard work as fundamentally important in their lives. They want to have good feelings about what they do, what they can achieve. You will, it's true, occasionally encounter an employee who would probably prefer backpacking through the woods. But for most people, work is central. They want to do it well.

The assertive-responsive approach described earlier is a healthy way to enter the counseling situation. The employee is probably not happy about the lack of effective performance. He or she brings certain concerns, resources, energies to the session. The other person would like a resolution, just as you would. In your counseling, the two of you sit down to find alternative behavior that will get better results than what you see now.

However, the counseling session may call for strong assertiveness on your part, instead of a combination of assertiveness-responsiveness. For example, you've counseled the employee previously on the same problem with no significant results. Now you know what the solution is; you don't have to work with the employee to find it. You insist on it—or else. This is the employee's last chance. Such firmness is legitimate when you believe that you have extended every bit of help to the employee. The employee's nonresponsiveness may not be your fault—or the employee's. The employee could be mismatched, or he or she might be so burdened with personal problems that on-the-job effectiveness is only remotely possible. Whatever, it is a time for your assertiveness, and your willingness to take extreme action if the improvement does not occur.

Scheduling the Interview

The best part of the day to arrange for the counseling session is in the morning, first thing. Don't give advance notice, say, the night before. The employee will have spent an anxious, sleepless, possibly angry, night. He or she will be in no mood to talk rationally with you. There are at least two reasons why early morning is ideal, if, indeed, any time is. First, you have all morning if you need it. Counseling must never be rushed. Don't schedule it when your time constraints are tight. A rushed counseling session may cause far more harm than good. Both of you need time to talk and reflect, to agree and to plan. You won't need all morning, of course, but the last thing you want is to sit there worrying about your next appointment when you should be listening.

The second reason why early morning is best is that it gives you the rest of the day to work with and interact with the employee on a normal basis. After all, you don't reject the employee, only certain behavior. The employee may leave your office wondering about being ostracized for a time. Later, as you walk by the employee and exchange a pleasantry, or stop to ask a work-related question, the employee knows that you are going to continue to treat him or her as a member of the work group. If the employee has further thoughts about the counseling and wants to discuss them with you or seeks clarification, you are available.

If you schedule the session near lunch hour, you create an undesirable time pressure. You'll also spoil lunch for the employee. The likelihood is that the employee will want to unburden some emotions over lunch with co-workers. You don't really need to have the misery and anger spread around. If you counseled early in the morning, some of the negative feelings will have drained off by noon.

Some managers hope to keep the employee from talking with other employees by scheduling the session late in the day or on Friday afternoon, when a whole weekend will pass before he can "poison" others' minds. The employee will seek out friends or family, and all will have sympathetic ears to his or her feelings. The employee's "side" gets reinforced. Or the employee will sit around, perhaps with a drink in hand, holding long imaginary conversations with you that become increasingly self-serving and justifying.

A regular day of work after the session will help convince your subordinate that the world did not stop turning at the time he or she entered your office.

If you can avoid it, don't give advance notice of the session. If you must schedule in advance, simply get his or her agreement to be available at a given time. Chances are you will have an anxious person to deal with. So keep the advance notice as short as possible.

Conduct the session in a private place where you can talk uninterruptedly. You don't want your secretary walking in and out; you don't want the phone ringing; and you certainly don't want another manager popping his or her head in the door. The deficient performance is the most important order of business. You owe both of you that consideration.

Avoid having a third person present if you can. You are in a power position which, in the employee's mind, puts him or her at a disadvantage. Having another person in the room intensifies that disadvantage as well as the employee's embarrassment. The employee will no doubt have the feeling that "They are ganging up on me." Consequently, the employee's talk will be highly defensive or minimal. Either is counterproductive.

Conducting the Interview

Following are some steps you may wish to use in your next counseling interview. They will help you to reduce some of your tension and, thereby, to lessen the employee's anxious feelings. The purpose of the interview is, of course, to correct a deficient performance problem, but you would also like the employee to come out of the session with self-esteem intact. You would also hope that the respect that the employee has for you is strengthened by the professional but human way you conduct the counseling.

1. State the problem. "There have been five unexplained absences in the past three weeks." "We agreed that you would make twenty new business calls each week, and you have failed to do so for the past six weeks." "You promised me that the deadline on the report would be met; yet you were three days late. This is the fourth important deadline you have missed."

Your preparation is indispensable. The subordinate has accepted a goal, a standard, a project, a responsibility and has failed to fulfill it. You have the evidence.

In stating the problem, and throughout the whole interview, stick to describing behavior and performance. Forget about talking in terms of attitudes and other intangibles that can't be seen and measured. Don't make judgments about motivations. For example, no matter how exasperated you might be, don't say something such as, "Apparently doing the best job you can is not one of your drives." Or, "You've made so many promises to me that you haven't kept that I have to wonder about your integrity." Whether the person is motivated to do a so-so job or to lie to you is not really the issue. The issue is that you expected a certain kind of performance, and you didn't get it. Furthermore, you had a right to expect it. You don't argue about that right, and you definitely do not wish to get bogged down in interpretations of motivations and attitudes.

Don't be so diplomatic that you run the risk of filtering out serious messages. For example, you would like to say, "Your work is clearly unacceptable, and it cannot continue this way." Perhaps you feel that you'd like to soften it, so you say, instead, "We both know that you can do better, and I don't think I'd be fair to either one of us if I didn't do everything I could to help you improve." What the employee may hear is that you worry that you may have let him or her down, or that you accept some of the responsibility for the problem. The fact is, and you'll learn this during the interview, you may indeed bear some responsibility. But don't open the door to that possibility at this point. And don't be anxious not to offend, lest you conceal the seriousness of the problem in the verbiage.

Your message must be unequivocal: "This is what we agreed you would do. You haven't done it, despite our talking about it. It must be done."

This is a time to be as straightforward and as objective as possible. For the moment, the evidence places the onus squarely on the employee's shoulders.

2. Get agreement on the deficiency. It's risky to proceed beyond this point without an agreement that you both have something important to talk about. Documentation is important, as stated earlier. Your assumptions can help you too. Adopt the assertive-responsive mode. Describe how you see the situation, and state your feelings about it. Ask the other person to tell you how he or she perceives the situation, and also how he or she feels about it. In many cases where the documentation is strong, and there have been previous conversations on the subject, you'll get some agreement that the employee recognizes the problem and is unhappy about it.

If you slide over this step without getting agreement, you probably won't make much further progress. There may be two reasons why the employee doesn't agree that there's a problem: (1) the person hasn't understood your previous feedback; and (2) the person doesn't regard your concern as justified. In the first case, which admittedly will be infrequent, you'd have to wonder about the communication between you. In the second, you have the evidence that the results were not as you require. If you run into continuing denial that a problem exists, you may have to say, "Perhaps you don't believe my standards or values are valid. I'm sorry about that. But I have a right to expect that my staff will work according to them. If you want to continue here, you'll have to accept them and abide by them whether you want to or not. Now I'm sure you agree that we have a problem, do you not?"

On that basis, you can continue. The employee may not be happy with your explanation, but he or she has to accept that you feel strongly about it.

In most situations, though, the employee enters your office well aware of the problem and uncomfortable about it.

3. Listen. Your subordinate probably has a story to tell. Let it be told without rebuttal. It costs you nothing but time to listen. But it can be very helpful if the session is to proceed. Also allow time for airing of negative feelings. A negative reaction is normal.

You don't have to agree with everything the subordinate has to say. If you sit it out, you're not necessarily endorsing the reasons, excuses, emotions, or any other negative responses. You are, however, treating the employee with respect and dignity. If you can't accept the person and the feelings, you will be hampered in arriving at a solution that is acceptable to you both.

In counseling, two kinds of listening are required: to things that are said and things that are not said. The employee may not volunteer all the necessary or helpful information. A salesman who is making too many service calls during prime selling time complains that he cannot ignore angry calls from unhappy customers. Why are they angry enough to demand immediate attention? Is it a deficiency in him, or in home office billings, or in delivery, or in product quality? A secretary who spends much time away from her desk may be unwilling to tell you about the sexual harassment she has undergone from one of the males.

Sometimes subordinates will assure you that they have accepted the counseling, that everything will be fine, that the changes will be made. They smile with their lips but not their eyes or their faces. In these cases, you may want to take more time to be sure that everything is in fact understood.

If the employee is not forthcoming with information that you suspect is there, try nondirective interviewing techniques. Encourage the employee to talk without leading him or her. Silence is a principal component of the technique. Silence creates tension, and people act to break that tension by talking. If you don't talk, the employee will. You can then offer support by saying, from time to time, "I see," "Yes, I can understand that," "Would you elaborate on that?"

Look at the employee. Eye contact is very important. Nod to show that you are listening. Occasionally, refer to something the employee has said to show that you have been paying attention: "So you feel that checking with the supervisor before making routine requisitions causes delays that may leave people without critical supplies?"

Listen carefully, because counseling is a learning opportunity for you. You could be getting feedback on conditions in the department about which you are not aware, on your effectiveness as a manager, on your communicating, on the covert acts of one of your supervisors, etc. Counseling often provides you with insights into how employees see their well-being, how they feel about what they are or are not doing, whether they believe they have a chance to achieve their personal goals through committing themselves to yours. If you don't learn something about the employee, the operation, the climate, the working conditions—and it doesn't have to be unpleasant knowledge, then it is possible the counseling has not been a complete success.

4. Consider extenuating circumstances. The employee's explanation of the deficiency and the reasons for it may be a rationalization. Then again, it may not be. There may have been some contributing factors over which the employee had no or, at the most, miminal control. For example:

• **Change of working conditions.** Working conditions may have changed since the task was defined, the objectives set, or the standards explained. The place where the work is done, the people involved, the flow of the work, the supervision, may be different now from what they were. Unless you are certain the employee's excuses are flimsy, check them out.

• **Insufficient knowledge or skill.** You might have picked the wrong person for the job. Or you chose a subordinate who has more will than skill. Now you may have to decide whether to replace him or her, or to provide training, help, or equipment to help get the job done.
• **Work load.** Without your being aware of it, the employee's work load may have changed, resulting in a disproportionate accountability. When you assigned the task, both you and the subordinate were confident of his or her ability to do it. But what happened subsequently to the total work load? You may have to reassign some of the person's responsibilities.

• **Conflict with co-workers.** The subordinate is clashing with others within your department or in another with which you must cooperate. It's possible that your subordinate contributes to the conflict, which has become a barrier to getting the work done. You may not be able to eliminate the conflict completely, but you have to find ways to help the employee to reduce his or her contributions to it.

• **Personal problems.** Here is a potential trap for you. Especially if the employee is valued, you may find it easy to get involved with his or her family, money, psychological, drinking problems. But it's doubtful that you have the expertise to deal with an employee's personal concerns. And your efforts to do so will divert you from your chief responsibility: to get the performance you require. Be prepared, therefore, to refer the employee to more capable help elsewhere. Don't forget, in your compassion, to emphasize the correction in performance that you must have.

5. Find a desirable alternative. The objective of counseling is to replace behavior that is ineffective with behavior that is effective. Now that you've gotten agreement that a problem exists, that goals are not being met or standards observed, you can say, "We both agree that this is not the way we want it. What can we do to make it right for both of us?" It's a much more attractive message than to keep saying, "What you're doing is wrong. Stop it." Keep the message positive. You are thus emphasizing the future and the partnership. A solution put forth by the employee that you can accept as workable is probably better than one you propose, because the employee will "own" it and work harder, in most cases, to implement it. That doesn't preclude your offering a solution, however, if the employee accepts it with some enthusiasm. The point is that a solution that you impose may not lead to a desirable change.

When you operate in the assertive-responsive mode, you encourage the employee to tell you how he or she thinks the job could be done within the context of that person's style and mode of operation. Furthermore, since it is the employee's solution, he or she will probably apply at least a bit more effort toward realizing it.

6. Get agreement on the alternative. The employee has joined with you in developing a solution or a desired alternative behavior. Repeat it to the employee and say something such as, "This is what we've agreed on. Is that right?" Don't assume agreement and understanding. When they want to avoid further embarrassment, people have a way of agreeing without understanding.

7. Design an action plan. How will it come about? When? By whom? It's possible that you will have to take certain actions, or provide resources, to help the employee carry out the plan. Or others might be involved in the behavior change. The important thing is that both of you know exactly what is to happen in order to improve the employee's performance.

8. Get the employee's perception of what has taken place. Again, you want to be sure that there is complete understanding. Ask the em-

ployee to summarize the discussion of the solution. You may wish to skip this step if the two of you sign a performance improvement document such as that on page 160.

9. Follow-through. Counseling is not a one-time event, as is on-the-spot criticism. If the problem is serious enough to require counseling, then it calls for follow-up. Monitor the action plan to see that it happens. If you don't, the word may get around that you really aren't serious. You undermine your credibility.

When the desired change takes place and you are satisfied, reinforce it. You increase the chances that the new behavior or way of performing will become permanent.

Of course, if the desired change does not occur, then further discussion between you and the employee is needed. You may have to adjust the action plan—try another approach, extend the timetable, apply more resources.

Or you may have to terminate the employee.

The Ordeal of Firing

You've given the employee every opportunity. You've criticized, evaluated, counseled. Perhaps you've even applied disciplinary measures. After all that, the employee's performance is not up to your standards. There are at least three reasons why you should consider firing. One has to do with the employee. Painful as it may be to admit, the employee is not in the right place. He or she is simply not suitable for the job, and vice versa. Terminating the employee may, in the long run, be best for that person.

A second reason in favor of termination involves fairness to your other subordinates. They have been suffering from a weak member of the team; sometimes they had to shoulder more work. Moreover, generally, it's an irritant to have someone in your group who is simply not effective. It's enough to prevent the formation of a really productive work team.

You are the third reason why you should consider terminating an ineffective subordinate. For one thing, your credibility is at stake. You can't expect to convince employees that they must give you their best when in their midst is one person who does not. For another, you create tension in yourself when you tolerate deficient performance. It is a problem that remains unresolved.

When you terminate deficient performers—after, of course, doing everything within reason to help them correct their performance, you reinforce a vital message: When you perform well in this department, you will be rewarded; when you perform poorly, you will be terminated.

Terminating is painful. You can't escape the fact. You can lessen the pain by following these recommendations:

• **Come right to the point.** No prefaces, no preambles. This is not the time for speeches or small talk. As quickly as you have the employee seated, tell the person why you've called him or her in. For example, "There's no easy way for me to say this. I'm going to have to terminate you (or, I have to ask for your resignation). I'm going to tell you why, and we can discuss this as much as you want. But, this is very important: The decision is irreversible. Nothing you will say to me can change the fact." Make sure the employee understands that you will not reverse yourself; otherwise you'll waste a lot of time hearing arguments in favor of reinstatement.

• **Give reasons.** And your reasons should be documented. The more facts and records you have, the safer you'll be. For one thing, the documentation makes it easier for the employee to accept this unpleasant truth. For another, it's harder for the employee in his or her anger to threaten legal action. "You and I agreed on three units per week (12 sales calls, 200 telephone calls, 100 letters, 50 new trainees per month), but your actual production has been only 60 percent of that. Despite our efforts, you haven't been able to increase your productivity, and it's a rate I cannot afford."

It's advisable to avoid sympathetic remarks such as, "It hasn't worked out," or, "I think you'd be better off somewhere else." Whatever the reason, the employee couldn't or wouldn't do the job, and you've been a conscientious manager in trying to help whichever way you could. Let it go at that.

• **Listen.** The employee is most likely in shock. He or she is not hearing well. Any long speeches on your part will, in all probability, be wasted. Give the other person a chance to speak up. Be patient. It's hard news for the subordinate to accept, even though he or she may have been expecting it. Expecting something and being prepared for it are quite different. This time is necessary for the subordinate.

However, if the talk turns abusive, you have a right to protect yourself from nastiness and insult. End the session by saying, "I know you're upset. I don't want you to say things you'll regret having said later. Let's talk again when you've had a chance to absorb this." Get up and open the door.

• **Have help ready.** After the employee has talked and calmed down a bit, define what help is available: an office and a telephone; outplacement counseling; group insurance for a time. It's usually a good idea to have prearranged an interview with a personnel specialist who can fill the employee in on what's available and what the person's status is. Keep the employee busy working on those matters that are important and can be helpful.

Make yourself available for further discussion. That's a function that some managers try to avoid, sometimes resorting to firing people on Friday afternoon. (Follow the recommendations for scheduling counseling; the same timing applies to firing.) But your accessibility and empathy can go a long way toward softening the bitterness that the terminated employee feels.

Counseling requires in you a combination of solid preparation, firmness, patience and understanding. Counseling is never a spontaneous event. You need to do your homework. You need to be firm. You cannot afford to be distracted from your objective. At the same time, you are patient and understanding. You have just put the employee through an unpleasant, even shocking, experience. Your humanness will help the employee to absorb that shock, perhaps more important, to grow from it.

Performance Improvement Plan

Employee's name: _____

1. Statement of the performance problem: _____

_____

_____

_____

_____

_____

_____

2. History of the performance problem.

   Previous dates on which the problem was discussed with employee:

   Critical feedback (dates and summary): _____

   _____

   _____

   _____

Appraisal feedback (dates and summary): _____

_____

_____

_____

_____

_____

Previous counseling on this problem (dates and summary): _____

_____

_____

_____

_____

_____

_____

Summary of agreed change in performance: _____

_____

_____

_____

_____

_____

Date of present counseling session: _____

Other persons present, if any: _____

_____   _____

3. Employee understands the problem as stated and agrees that it should be discussed.   Yes _____   No _____

If no, summarize employee's objection: _____

_____

_____

_____

_____

List documentation and other supporting evidence presented: _____

_____

_____

_____

_____

_____

4. I listened fully to employee's explanation: _____

5. I considered the following extenuating factors that have contributed to the problem:

_____

_____

_____

_____

_____

_____

The following actions will be taken to alter the factors or to change circumstances:

_____

_____

_____

_____

Who will take the action? _____

By when will the action be taken? _____

6. I have referred the employee for further counseling to the following: _____

_____

_____

7. I have attempted to enlist the employee's aid in finding an alternative or

solution: _____

Description of the solution:

_____

_____

_____

_____

_____

8. Description of the steps to be taken to accomplish the solution and by

whom:

a. _____

By: _____

b. _____

By: _____

c. _____

By: _____

Target date(s) for completion (by steps if necessary): _____

_____

_____

_____

_____

_____

9. Follow-through.

Dates of review: _____

_____

_____

10. Action recommended if the change does not occur:

_____

_____

_____

_____

_____   _____
       Manager's signature   Employee's signature

NOTE: If employee declines to sign, please explain:

_____

_____

_____

_____

Sample Counseling Interviews

Following is a counseling interview. As you read through the exchange between the manager and his subordinate supervisor, you may want to make notes in the margin about what you think is a good technique on the part of the manager or a bad one. When you finish, you can compare your analysis with the one at the end.

Manager: Come in, John. It's good to see you. Have a chair. How are you this morning?

Subordinate: Fine, Steve. And yourself?

Manager: Pretty good for an old guy. I was thinking about having some coffee. Would you like some? No? Lisa, would you please bring me a cup of coffee? Thanks. Let me shut the door. I thought we might have a little chat about the way things are going. It's been a while since you and I got together. How *are* things going?

Subordinate: Things are going fine, I guess.

Manager: Would you say that you have any unresolved problems that need to be talked about? Oh, Lisa. Thanks for the coffee. Where was I?

Subordinate: You were talking about unresolved problems. I don't think so. Oh, you know, there are always those little things that crop up from day to day. Kind of petty, really.

Manager: Hm.

Subordinate: Have you got something on your mind, Steve?

Manager: Well, let me put it this way. Do you feel confident that you are getting what you want from your people?

Subordinate: Sure I do. My people work very well for me.

Manager: I know they do, John. But other people might have a different perception of how hard they work for you.

Subordinate: How could they?

Manager: They could by walking through your department at certain times. For example, I've been there at quarter after nine, and half of the offices are empty. That's true of other parts of the day. I guess what I'm trying to say is that your folks aren't taking the company policy very seriously.

Subordinate: You mean that recent memo?

Manager: Sure. Top management sent the memo for a reason. They want people to work from nine to five, with an hour for lunch. Your people don't seem to.

Subordinate: They work, Steve; they work damned hard.

Manager: I'm sure they do. But when the brass walk through and see so many people away, they wonder.

Subordinate: What's more important, show or substance?

Manager: It's not that easy, John. Get around to the other departments. You'll see people at their desks at nine. Not ten after. Nine.

Subordinate: Steve, how can you ask me to take that memo seriously? What's important is the work. These little piddly rules are just that. What's going on? Management doesn't have enough to do? Someone is bored and says to himself, "I'll write a memo."

Manager: Don't get upset, John. Yes, Lisa? Rob Leinowitz? Okay, I'll take it. Excuse me, John, while I take this call. Just stay put.

(A few minutes pass)

Manager: Sorry about that. I know that rules sometimes seem a little silly, but not to some people. Those people take their rules seriously. They also have something to say about whether you and I keep our jobs.

Subordinate: Look, Steve, my people are very productive. Do you have a problem with my department's output?

Manager: No.

Subordinate: Do you know why? Because when I took the job of heading the department, I made a bargain with them. We didn't put it in words. It just developed. I'd stay out of their way, and they'd do the work. Not only is our productivity high, but my absenteeism is the lowest of any department I know. Isn't that true? And turnover, forget it. That's because I stay off their backs.

Manager: You're right that you have a fine group of people. But we have rules, and those rules have to be followed. Otherwise, you and I are both going to hear about it.

Subordinate: And do you know what's going to happen when I enforce those silly little rules? Morale is going to drop. People are going to give me what they have to. Productivity is going right to where it was when I took over. It will be enough to keep everyone out of trouble. All for the sake of a few minutes in the morning and during the day. "We don't care whether you work or not, just be there at your desks."

Manager: I think you're exaggerating, John. I think they'll adapt fine. But you're going to have to enforce the rules. I want you to know I'm serious about this. After

all, I've spoken to you about this before.

Subordinate: Oh, I know, Steve, but I didn't think the way you put it was that serious.

Manager: In effect, this is your second warning. I'm going to have to insist that you take the proper action.

Subordinate: All right. I'll tell them that from now on, nine-to-five, one hour for lunch.

ANALYSIS: A counseling session is a serious occasion. The manager, Steve, trivialized the occasion by four actions. First, he characterized the meeting as a chat, as a casual meeting after a long time of not getting together. Second, he offered coffee and asked his assistant to bring some, guaranteeing they would be disturbed when she returned. It's probably not a good idea to offer coffee to the subordinate, since such an offer is more social than is desirable on such an occasion. Third, he took the phone call, again interrupting the interview and leaving his subordinate, John, to deal with his own anger during the minutes Steve was on the phone. Fourth, he waited until the very end of the interview to remind John that he had spoken to him earlier about the tardiness of his people.

But there are some other mistakes Steve made. At the beginning, he should have stated clearly what he regarded the problem to be. Instead, he tried to wheedle a self-confession out of his subordinate: "Would you say that you have any unresolved problems that need to be talked about?" Presumably it would have been much easier if John had acknowledged the tardiness. Another error involves Steve's lack of willingness to take responsibility for the policy. He puts the responsibility on higher management. He doesn't say, "I'm your manager, and it is important to me that you follow the dictates of the memo." Then he compares Steve's department with the others: *They're* all at work when they should be. Why can't your people do the same?

Steve makes no real effort to help John understand that there is a problem that would be solved by John's enforcement of the rules. John sees no problem: His implicit bargain is paying off in higher productivity.

Finally, the manager seems not to want to deal with John's resentment. He tells his subordinate not to "get upset." Later he tries to quiet him by suggesting that his emotions are exaggerated. The result very likely is that John will carry his resentment out of the office back to his department. John will make the announcement and will enforce the rules unhappily. Nothing good will come from the session. Steve will be bewildered by the sad turn of events. He will not, of course, ascribe a role to himself in the process.

Following is another counseling interview. Repeat the process as in the previous interview and compare your analysis at the end.

Manager: Come in, Susan. Shut the door and have a seat.
Subordinate: You wanted to see me?
Manager: Yes. I think you know what it's all about. I've spoken to you before about your coming in late and leaving early. Do you remember?
Subordinate: Yes.
Manager: Well, you're still doing it. Last time when we talked, I thought we had an agreement. Didn't we?
Subordinate: I guess so.
Manager: What do you mean, Susan? Did we or didn't we?
Subordinate: I said I'd do the best I could.
Manager: That's not what you said.
Subordinate: Well, I can only do what I can do.
Manager: I thought I made it clear that this is something you have to do.
Subordinate: I have an old car and it keeps breaking down.
Manager: Can't you get it fixed?
Subordinate: I take it to this friend of my cousin's. He doesn't charge so much. And he tells me that he's fixed it, but then it breaks down again.
Manager: Maybe you'd better get a new mechanic.
Subordinate: Do you know how much they cost these days?
Manager: Well, then, get a new car.
Subordinate: Mr. Wright, I can't afford to go out and buy a new car on what I make here.
Manager: We pay you very well for your level of position. And I don't think you'll find anything better at any other company in this area.
Subordinate: I don't seem to be able to make ends meet.
Manager: What are you going to do about that car?
Subordinate: I don't know. I guess I'll just have to do the best I can.
Manager: What does that mean?
Subordinate: Well, I'll take it back to get it fixed. Where I'm going to find the money, I don't know.
Manager: Is your car the reason you sometimes leave here a half hour early?

Subordinate: That's my baby-sitter. She has a dance class sometimes that she has to leave early for, and I have to be home when she leaves.

Manager: For her dance class?

Subordinate: Yes.

Manager: Well, Susan, what are we going to do about our problems?

Subordinate: As I said, I'll try to get the car fixed.

Manager: Don't forget, I want you in here on time every morning. It's not fair to your co-workers. Furthermore, I don't see why we have to suffer because your sitter has a dance class. Don't you agree?

Subordinate: I guess so.

Manager: That's not good enough. I'm going to note in your record that this is the third time that we have discussed this problem, and that you have promised to correct your tardiness and your leaving early in the afternoon. Do you understand?

Subordinate: Yes.

Manager: Are we in agreement?

Subordinate: Yes.

Manager: You're a good worker. I don't want to lose you.

Subordinate: Thank you.

ANALYSIS: This manager is faced with an employee who is proficient at sidetracking and seeming to promise what she really doesn't. In counseling, it is essential for the manager to maintain control of the interview from start to finish. This manager began to lose control when the subordinate reminded him that she had an old car that "keeps breaking down," and he responded with "Can't you get it fixed?" A proper response would have been, "I'm sorry to hear that. But I have a problem. I want you to come in on time, and

you don't do that." Unfortunately, she drags him further afield. Or more correctly, he lets himself be side-tracked. First, he suggests that she get herself a new mechanic, then a new car. The latter recommendation opens the door to her complaining about the money she earns. His reaction is very defensive, none of which answers his problem: He wants her to work a full day, and she has all sorts of reasons why she can't. The reasons are not really for him to worry about. They are her concern. But she "sells" them to him. He suggests answers.

He started the interview with the appropriate solemnity and single-mindedness. He did not, however, get her agreement that her behavior is a problem. She seems to have the attitude that her problems are beyond her to solve. There was no negative reaction, suggesting that emotionally she wasn't really affected by the interview.

When he asked, "What are we going to do about our problems?" he further blurred issues. He would have been better advised to put it this way, "Yes, I can see you have a problem. But so do I. I expect mine to be solved if you are to remain working here. How are you going to solve my problem?" That should have been his track from which he refused to depart. "I have a problem. I want it solved." He should have resolutely refused to discuss her car and baby-sitter problems. He should have acknowledged them, true, but continued to remind her of what the interview was all about.

He says that her conduct is not fair to her co-workers. Managers often resort to this cop-out. The fact is, he needs her to work a full day. He wants that. He must accept responsibility that his standards are what count, not those of other employees.

Finally, he let her go without an action plan, without a commitment. She entered his office, seemingly without responsibility for her behavior. She left the same way.

Here is a third counseling interview for your analysis.

Manager: Jane, hello. Please come in and sit down. I asked you to come by because I have a problem I think we ought to discuss.

Subordinate: What's that?

Manager: I'd have thought you already knew. You were out of the office yesterday afternoon. Two of your supervisors ran into some heavy problems. They needed you, but they didn't know where you were.

Subordinate: I was in the field, looking at some new properties.

Manager: Why didn't they know about it?

Subordinate: I mentioned it to my assistant.

Manager: She didn't seem to know about it. If they'd all known you were in the field, they might have been able to contact you. Or at least they wouldn't have spent all that time looking for you or waiting for you to come back.

Subordinate: I'm sorry about the mix-up, but when I came in this morning we straightened things out. I talked with my supervisors, and we're on the right track now.

Manager: I think you're lucky. Things could be picked up and put together. But I don't think that quite takes care of my problem. You were out, and no one knew where you were. I've talked with you before about other times you disappeared. I thought you understood how serious it can be for your supervisors if they can't come to you when they get into trouble with tenants. For example, one man was unruly yesterday, and they were afraid they should ask for the police. That's the kind of decision you should make. At any rate, they needed the support of their manager, who wasn't to be found.

Subordinate: It was a mix-up, and I don't understand why you're making a big fuss about it. I told you, I told my assistant that I would be in the field. Anyway, the problems are cleared up; no damage was done.

Manager: Except to my trust.

Subordinate: Why are you coming down so hard on me? Is it because all those rumors about my having an affair with Bernard? Was he out too?

Manager: He was out too, but that is something else.

Subordinate: So you think the two of us were shacked up in a hotel room?

Manager: Jane, let's stay on the subject. You know the policy. Managers going into the field have to alert all interested parties, leave locations and numbers, if possible, where they can be reached. You didn't follow the policy. What's worse, you and I have talked about this twice previously, and you agreed with me that it should not happen again. Isn't that correct?

Subordinate: Yes, you're right, but Carole sometimes goes out without following policy and I don't hear you sitting on her. Why do I get singled out?

Manager: I didn't ask you here to talk about Carole. We're talking about you.

Subordinate: All right, but I think you can understand why I believe it was all those rumors about Bernard and me that got me into trouble.

Manager: Once and for all, Jane, I really don't care about your relationship, if any, with Bernard. I only care about what goes on here. Am I right in saying that you understand the policy and that you previously agreed to follow it?

Subordinate: Yes.

Manager: How are you going to prevent this from happening again?

Subordinate: I'll tell my assistant where I can be found.

Manager: What about your supervisors?

Subordinate: Them too.

Manager: One other thing, Jane. If you forget to follow this procedure again, I won't be likely to sit down and talk with you again about it. I'll be thinking about taking action.

Subordinate: Such as?

Manager: One option I have is demotion. I could drop you down to supervisor.

Subordinate: Charlotte, would you honestly do that after all the time I've worked for you?

Manager: I would rather not. But you control the situation, you know. Do this thing right, and we don't have to worry about it. Before you leave, one more time: When you go into the field from now on, whom will you notify?

Subordinate: My assistant and my supervisors. And I'll tell them how they can locate me.

ANALYSIS: This is nearly a model for an effective counseling interview. From the outset, the manager kept control of the interview process. She stated the problem and refused to be sidetracked by: (1) Jane's alleged relationship with a co-worker; and (2) Carole's reported violating of policy. She made sure that Jane understood the problem and the seriousness of it. She reminded Jane that they had discussed similar problem behavior twice before. She got an agreement from Jane as to what she would do in the future when she went into the field. She closed the session with having Jane repeat her perception of what had gone on, and she let Jane know, unequivocally, that there would be no further counseling. Any further action would be disciplinary, possibly severe.

Here is the fourth and final counseling interview for your analysis:

Manager: Come in, Phil. Have a seat. I thought it was time you and I had a chat, now that I've taken over the department from Mac.

Subordinate: I think we all knew it would be you, Mike.

Manager: Well, there were some strong hints from above. Anyway, I have some serious matters I'd like to discuss with you, Phil.

Subordinate: What, Mike? Is something wrong?

Manager: Frankly, yes. Uh, well, there's no easy way to put it. I've been working with you for some time now, Phil, and I have to tell you that your work is unacceptable.

Subordinate: What? Mike, I've been here eighteen years. No one has ever said that to me before.

Manager: Well, I'm saying it to you now. You're just not doing the kind of work I want.

Subordinate: I do good work. Why, after all this time, do you tell me it's not?

Manager: I've always felt this way, but I wasn't in charge.

Subordinate: Mac always liked my copy.

Manager: I'm not sure. When I took over, he told me that he thought you might have gone stale.

Subordinate: But he never said that. Not to me.

Manager: It's hard for me to believe that this comes as a big surprise to you. After all, I've sat in on lots of editorial meetings when your copy was severely criticized by the other editors. Surely you're not going to deny that.

Subordinate: I won't. But why should I accept their word as superior? My work is good. I know it. I'm the only one here who writes the kind of thing I write, and our publications need it.

Manager: Phil, there's little point in dragging this out and making it more painful than it is already. I have to tell you: I want you to follow these criteria. I've written them down.

Subordinate: You're the boss. This is what you want. This is what you'll get.

ANALYSIS: This manager is in deep trouble from the outset. He started the counseling session with no documentation. Before resorting to counseling, he should have made it very clear what he expected from Phil and then given the subordinate a chance to act on those standards. Instead, he initiates a counseling interview, at the conclusion of which he hands Phil criteria to be followed in his future writing.

When Phil resists his evaluation of his copy, the manager quotes his predecessor, Mac, as saying "He thought you might have gone stale." Not only is it unfair to quote someone else in a counseling interview as authority, this statement could mean lots of things. It is not specific enough to constitute good feedback. When the manager encounters more resistance, he summons up informal peer evaluations that have occurred in editorial meetings. The manager's lack of preparation and his ignoring preliminary steps (such as establishing standards and giving informal feedback) have created an embarrassing situation from which neither person can emerge feeling good.

The manager doesn't listen. The subordinate makes a point that he is the only person writing a type of copy that he, Phil, thinks the publications need. Whether or not Mike agrees, he should get Phil's thinking on that need. Obviously, Mike is not interested. He presses his point, regardless of Phil's response. Phil promises to give Mike what he wants, but the spirit is obviously lacking. Mike has moved an experienced employee from deficiency to probable demotivation.

Reviewing Your Counseling Expertise

	Yes	No	Not Sure
1. Counseling is needed when a performance problem threatens to seriously disrupt the employee's productivity or that of others.	_____	_____	_____
2. Counseling that is delayed can create tension and stress in both you and the subordinate.	_____	_____	_____

	Yes	No	Not Sure
3. Employees who sense they are not competent or productive usually accept counseling.	_____	_____	_____
4. It's important to approach counseling with the attitude that the employee's performance is "on trial," not the employee.	_____	_____	_____
5. You are more effective in counseling when you believe you can persuade the employee to agree to improve performance.	_____	_____	_____
6. Performance appraisal time is usually the best time for counseling.	_____	_____	_____
7. Counseling can be cost-effective because salvaging an employee is often cheaper than recruiting a replacement.	_____	_____	_____
8. When an employee is failing or turning in an unsatisfactory performance, you have an obligation to take every reasonable step to help that employee.	_____	_____	_____
9. When you counsel an employee, you reassure others who want to believe that you would help them out of a performance problem.	_____	_____	_____
10. Employees who fail often should be gotten rid of quickly or else they will demotivate and demoralize others.	_____	_____	_____
11. Employees who perform deficiently may not know what they are supposed to do or how to do it.	_____	_____	_____
12. The more documentation or evidence of an employee's performance problems you have, the less stress you'll probably feel when counseling him or her.	_____	_____	_____
13. You should never counsel when you are feeling angry with the employee.	_____	_____	_____

	Yes	No	Not Sure
14. If the employee shows negative feelings at being counseled, you are right to say "Don't get emotional."	_____	_____	_____
15. Reasonable employees do not have negative reactions to your counseling and should be able to accept it.	_____	_____	_____
16. It is helpful to identify employee attitudes that you believe contribute to poor performance.	_____	_____	_____
17. To get the employee to accept your counseling, do everything possible to avoid offending the person.	_____	_____	_____
18. It's helpful for you to listen to the employee's reactions or explanations, even though you don't agree with everything the person says.	_____	_____	_____
19. When the employee does not volunteer the information you need, be patient and use a nondirective approach.	_____	_____	_____
20. If you don't learn something about the employee, the operation, and working conditions in the counseling interview, it is possible that the counseling has not been a complete success.	_____	_____	_____
21. There may be extenuating circumstances to explain at least part of the employee's performance deficiency, and you should pledge yourself to take quick, effective action to remove such conditions or barriers.	_____	_____	_____
22. When an employee's performance deficiency is caused by personal problems, you should try to understand what the problems are before you try to counsel.	_____	_____	_____

	Yes	No	Not Sure
23. When you are in the assertive-responsive mode, you encourage the employee to come up with a solution he or she feels responsible to carry out.	_____	_____	_____
24. When you agree on a solution, you can regard the counseling as successful.	_____	_____	_____
25. When the desired change takes place, you should reinforce it.	_____	_____	_____
26. The best time for counseling is late in the day, so the employee has plenty of time to think about it at home that evening.	_____	_____	_____
27. Another good time to schedule counseling is just before lunch. This gives the employee time to get away from the office before resuming work.	_____	_____	_____
28. It's a good idea to invite your manager for the session so as to impress the employee with your seriousness.	_____	_____	_____
29. When more than one performance problem is involved, it is generally a good idea to pick the one that has the higher priority.	_____	_____	_____
30. If you do not impress the employee with one problem, have another as a back-up just in case.	_____	_____	_____
31. If you have to fire an employee, it's best to do it early in the day and week.	_____	_____	_____
32. When you fire, be ready to offer whatever help and counsel you or the organization can.	_____	_____	_____
33. When the deficiency or problem that brought about the termination is the employee's, don't let him or her try to assign the blame elsewhere.	_____	_____	_____
34. If you do not terminate an employee who will not or cannot work according to your standards, you risk demotivating others who do.	_____	_____	_____

	Yes	No	Not Sure
35. Compassion is an acceptable emotion for you to have in a counseling session, so long as it does not prevent you from taking appropriate actions.	_____	_____	_____
36. Generally, empathy is more desirable in the counselor than sympathy.	_____	_____	_____
37. Patience is an essential characteristic of an effective counselor.	_____	_____	_____

Answers to Counseling Review

1. Yes
2. Yes
3. Yes
4. Yes
5. Yes
6. Not sure. Counsel only if the seriousness of the problem becomes apparent at the time of the appraisal. Otherwise, schedule the counseling when the problem becomes clear. Don't wait for appraisal time. Appraisals should have as few surprises for the employee as possible.
7. Yes
8. Yes
9. Yes
10. Yes
11. Yes
12. Yes
13. Yes
14. No. Expect a negative reaction, and let it be expressed.
15. Not sure. Many people will have initial negative reactions, but some may not.
16. No. Forget attitudes; stick to behavior.
17. No. Even if you risk offending the employee in order to counsel effectively, you must counsel in the way that will get best results.
18. Yes
19. Yes
20. Yes
21. Not sure. You may want to enlist the employee's aid in doing so, as in the case of personal problems.
22. Not sure. You may not want to get deeply involved in the details of a personal problem. And you probably aren't qualified to deal with them anyway.
23. Yes
24. Not sure. You should also check to make sure the employee understands the agreement.
25. Yes
26. No
27. No
28. No. No one else should be present unless that person plays an essential role.
29. Yes
30. No
31. Yes
32. Yes
33. Yes
34. Yes
35. Yes
36. Yes
37. Yes

Chapter Eight

How to Get More of What You Want from Your Meeting

When you hold a meeting with your work group or a portion of it, you're usually looking for their help in dealing with a departmental issue, in solving a problem, or in making a decision. That's your short-term objective. You have a long-term goal, which is to build a more effective group. The behaviors you encourage in a meeting can carry over to outside the conference room. Actually, the meeting is one of the best means of building a team, since, if your department is typical, your people may spend anywhere from one-third to one-half of their time in conferences.

As a manager wishing to share your leadership and help your group to greater productivity, you want to avoid the autocratic approach of designing a rigid, perhaps tight, agenda and presiding in the manner of a drill sergeant. At the same time, you hardly want to go the laissez-faire route by scheduling an open-ended meeting with little or no agenda and waiting for something to happen.

The key to effective problem-solving or decision-making meetings —and to building a team—lies somewhere between rigidly controlling the process and abdicating all responsibility for it. You are more likely to get what you want from a meeting if you pay close attention to your planning; are aware of, and use, direct and indirect, formal and informal, leadership roles; and understand special techniques that help promote consensus.

Consensus is recommended over majority vote, for at least three reasons: First, everyone has a chance to have a say. No one gets left out of the process. Second, with consensus, you are likely to develop more options because you are willing to include everyone and take the time. Third, in a consensus decision, people don't just go along with the decision; they have input into it and usually believe it is the best they could have come up with. Thus they are committed to carrying it out. The decision-making doesn't stop at the door to the conference room.

The following self-quiz will help you analyze your meeting effectiveness.

How Effective is Your Meetings Management?

	Frequently	Occasionally	Rarely
1. In my department people complain that they spend a great deal of time in meetings.	_____	_____	_____
2. People drift in late so that our meetings do not get started on time.	_____	_____	_____
3. During the first fifteen minutes or more, we seem to have problems getting agreement on the agenda.	_____	_____	_____
4. There is one person or a small group who dominate meetings from the outset and whose ideas are accepted by the group.	_____	_____	_____
5. It is difficult to get a hearing on new ideas because of negativism and resistance.	_____	_____	_____
6. People seem to devote more energy to finding out what is wrong with an idea than what is good.	_____	_____	_____
7. It is hard to get most participants to open up and offer their ideas or possible solutions.	_____	_____	_____
8. Some people are quiet and do not contribute to the discussions.	_____	_____	_____
9. I suspect that in our meetings we do not develop all of the options of courses of action that we might.	_____	_____	_____
10. Our meetings seem to drift, and people arrive at a decision or solution only in the last few minutes.	_____	_____	_____
11. I think our decisions are the product of frustration and time pressure, or a desire to close out the meeting.	_____	_____	_____

	Frequently	**Occasionally**	**Rarely**
12. Our decisions are arrived at by majority vote.	_____	_____	_____
13. Our meetings tend to run longer than I plan or want.	_____	_____	_____
14. Some people in our meetings clash with others and I'm not sure exactly what the conflict is all about.	_____	_____	_____
15. One or more participants can be counted on to make long rambling speeches that bore most others.	_____	_____	_____
16. There seems to be more competitiveness than cooperation among the members of my group.	_____	_____	_____
17. After meetings, participants seem to spend much time rehashing what went on in the meetings.	_____	_____	_____
18. After decisions are made, there is confusion about what exactly was decided.	_____	_____	_____
19. Our wrangling over the same issues is carried from one meeting to another.	_____	_____	_____
20. People charged with carrying out a decision or solution don't, but offer the explanation that they were not sure what was to be done or that they were charged with doing it.	_____	_____	_____
21. There is much talking in our meetings about issues that have little or nothing to do with the meeting agenda.	_____	_____	_____
22. Some people complain that their contributions are not taken seriously by the rest of the group.	_____	_____	_____
23. I have heard some subordinates complain that they do not think it is wise to open up and express what is really on their minds, either about the issues being discussed or the way the meetings are going.	_____	_____	_____
24. The tension in our meetings is discernible and lasting.	_____	_____	_____

	Frequently	Occasionally	Rarely
25. People seem to be quick to disagree with a contribution even before they have enough information to evaluate it properly.	_____	_____	_____
26. People do a lot of interrupting of others in meetings.	_____	_____	_____
27. People offer ideas and suggestions that are ignored by everyone else.	_____	_____	_____
28. Much meeting time is taken up with arguments about what people really said or interpretations of what they said.	_____	_____	_____
29. Some people are successful in putting others down in meetings.	_____	_____	_____

Analyzing Your Meetings Management Effectiveness

The twenty-nine questions that you have just worked with represent a meeting's pathology. Any question that you answered with "frequently" represents a possible impediment to your effectiveness in conducting meetings. You should consider it a red flag demanding immediate attention. Questions that you answered with "occasionally" are yellow flags calling for precautions on your part. Ignoring them has both a short-term and long-term consequence. For the moment, you are permitting barriers to a fully functioning meeting. You are also encouraging behavior that eventually will grow into a serious, frequent problem.

Use the following analysis to point you in the direction of corrective action.

1. What people are really complaining about is that they cannot see justification for spending all that time. The time spent is very likely disproportionate to the results achieved. In the pages following, you will find recommendations to help you cut down on the time actually spent around the conference table, enabling you to accomplish more in the time you do spend.

2. When people frequently arrive late, they are expressing negative feelings: They are reluctant to be there; they probably don't take the meeting seriously; or their lateness is a power ploy. An effective and easy way to head off counterproductive behavior is to consistently make a point of starting on time. If you don't, you reinforce the very behavior you don't want. Once the knowledge that you start promptly gets around, most of your laggards will be on time. As for those imposing some power on you with "fashionably" late entrances, your best move is to do nothing. Just ignore them. Eventually, they will realize that they are not achieving anything but the reputation for being disruptive. Remember, if you make any sort of welcome to a latecomer, you are rewarding behavior you don't want. If they apologize but continue to come in late, ignore the apology.

3. When meetings are slow to get going, the answer usually can be found in general confusion over what is to be discussed. What are the objectives of the meeting? It's helpful to alert people to the reason for the meeting before they arrive. They come better prepared. They may even have done some helpful thinking beforehand that will facilitate a solution. Your first step, after opening the session, is to state the problem and the objectives. It is common in the first stage of a meeting for the group to be dependent on the leader. Respond to that need by making it clear what is to be done and taking responsibility for starting the process. Then, as the group becomes more confident and effective, relinquish the controls gradually.

4. The dominator continues to dominate if he or she gets away with it. But if the dominator is successful, it usually means that you are not enjoying other resources that the group has to offer. Also, the dominator may be filling a vacuum in leadership that you may be creating. In the face of domination, many people will simply give up. "Why bother?" they will ask. If you make it possible and rewarding for others to contribute, they will help you to diminish the domination.

5. Opening the meeting up to new ideas and encouraging support for their expression are leadership functions, to be performed by the actual, former leader and by others exercising informal leadership. One relatively easy way to get ideas on record without their encountering a wall of resistance is to set aside a portion early in every meeting when each person is asked to contribute his or her ideas without fear of criticism. During the so-called round robin, ideas are recorded and no evaluating is permitted until afterwards. This technique won't eliminate all resistance and negativism, but it will permit the budding of new ideas before they are trampled on.

6. There are a number of reasons why people spend so much energy being negative, but most of them can be dealt with by supportive leadership. You can provide this kind of leadership by staying with the positive as much as possible: For example, "What do you like about this approach? What do you think needs to be done to make such an idea work?" Nay-saying is a relatively simple function. It doesn't require much skill. Help your group members to build more confidence in their abilities to work together. Don't let decisions be made too fast, before all aspects of a solution are considered. And reward people for taking risks in the group. Gradually, you'll reduce the power of the naysayer, who can function only when people are uncertain, confused, and unwilling to take chances.

7. People tend to do what they feel rewarded for doing. If you make it possible for them to contribute to the discussion and let them know how much you appreciate their having done so, you'll achieve more participation.

8. Encourage them to look for ways in which they can make a contribution and even exercise an informal leadership role. Then, make sure they are not dominated by more vocal, assertive members of the group.

9. Groups have a tendency to close out discussion early in the deliberation and push for a decision, usually the first solution that seems feasible. It may not, however, be the best. Leadership keeps the discussion going until more options are considered. Also, if you insist on a con-

sensus decision instead of a majority decision, you will have a better chance of developing a greater number of options.

10. Leadership, both formal and informal, that is, by you and by the other members of the group, is the key to keeping the session on track. A decision that is made out of frustration or desperation is probably not a good one.

11. It is often more desirable to schedule a follow-up meeting to complete the decision-making process than to close too early.

12. It's probable that most decisions do reflect the will of the majority. The disadvantages of majority decisions are twofold: First, the group may push for a majority decision without making sure that everyone is heard from, leaving the field to the strongest, but not necessarily the wisest, segment of the group; and second, people who find themselves in the minority may not feel strongly committed to carrying out the decision.

13. Good meetings management requires definite time boundaries. As was covered earlier, starting a meeting on time is important. Setting a closing time limit is just as important. If the time constraints are reasonable (people consider that the job *could* be completed in the time specified), they may facilitate the success of the group in reaching its objective. People will assume a timekeeping role. They will place limits on rambling, dominating, personal disputes, etc. The time limit should reflect the fact that most people can concentrate effectively only for relatively short periods of time, probably, for the majority, no more than ninety minutes.

14. If the reasons for conflicts and the issues involved are not clear, then you may have to look for hidden agendas or problems that originate outside the meeting room. In the case of hidden agendas, people are simply not leveling with the group as to what they really want in and from the group. Other members of the group respond to convert agendas with anger, suspicion, or confusion. Sometimes, members of the group will bring their continuing disputes with one another into the conference and inflict those disputes on everyone else.

15. People who ramble and take the group's time unnecessarily should be required to relate what they are saying to the objectives of the group. Feel free to stop a rambler by saying, "I'm not sure I understand how what you are saying applies to the discussion. Would you make that clear to us?" You may have to insist on it. You are forcing a mental discipline on a person who is not accustomed to it. But it's for the success of the group's efforts that you do.

16. If members of a group do not clearly understand or accept the objectives of the group, they will compete with one another to achieve their own respective objectives rather than work to accomplish what is important to the group. Make the objectives clear and encourage people to support one another by recognizing each act of support. A little competitiveness is fine, but it should not be at the expense of someone else's effectiveness. Behaviors that shut others off, that prevent their making contributions, or that put down their contributions should not be tolerated.

17. If there are extensive meetings after meetings, it usually indicates that people's personal objectives are not achieved in the meetings, that they don't accept what went on, and that they probably weren't upfront in their behavior in the group. It can

also mean that your meeting had a subgroup that dominated and prevented others from doing the job they wanted to do.

18. To prevent confusion about what was decided, you may have to check the participants' understanding of what has been resolved and how committed they are to the decision. This should, of course, be accomplished prior to adjournment.

19. Unresolved issues that are carried from one meeting to another are disruptive. They also prevent people from getting on with the work that has to be done. Actually, people may resort to rehashing the same issues when they want to avoid doing the more appropriate work. Ask yourself why they may be avoiding the proper work? Is it risk? Can you reduce the risk? Or have they simply not bought the previous resolution? If so, you'll want to find out why. Are they continuing to bring in issues and personal conflicts from the outside? Your leadership in the group should restrict such inappropriate conflict. Outside the group, you should work at managing the conflict through interviews with the disputants.

20. When people do not carry out the decision and claim they didn't understand the *what* or *who* of it, you have a clear indication that you have to take time to check people's understanding and commitment before you leave the conference table.

21. It is the responsibility of meeting participants to restrict their discussions and comments to the group's business. If you believe people are getting off the track, exercise your rights as a leader to require them to make the connection between what you want done and what they are doing.

22. It's possible that some contributions are not being taken seriously by the group. Ask yourself why not.

Are people not listening or responding? Are some participants ignoring others' contributions to assert their own? Or are some participants simply ineffective? If so, what can you do as manager to help them be more effective? You don't want to waste their resources. You may have to prepare them more than you would the others. You may have to coach them in advance. You might want to look for areas of the discussion in which you believe these people can make good contributions and then encourage them to speak out. Be sure that when these people do speak out, they receive acknowledgment and encouragement.

23. When people don't level in a group, the message is that they don't trust the group. They may be afraid that their opinions will be belittled or ignored. They may worry about being "punished" if they say something that is at odds with more vocal or assertive fellow workers. The person who fears saying what is on his or her mind is a wasted resource. Furthermore, this may be an indication that working conditions in the group are not what they should be, that the group is ineffective.

24. There is likely to be tension in any group that is working hard to resolve an issue. After all, people have their own perspectives and agendas, and they are trying to get some personal achievement and satisfaction in helping the group accomplish its objectives. Consequently, there will be some competitiveness, but the competition should be confined to working through the issues. When feelings run high over personalities, then you must direct them back to issues. As the group begins to achieve some success in dealing with the issues, the tension and anger will fade. If they do not fade, you may have to ask the people who feel nega-

tively to express their tensions and ask for help from the group in taking care of what has apparently not been resolved—a person's anger over another's behavior or dissatisfaction with the group's work on issues.

25. There are good psychological explanations for why people take negative stances even before they are sure what they disagree with, but the antidote is uncomplicated. You or some other member of the group have to intervene. First, you make sure that the original contributor has the opportunity to give whatever information he or she wants on the table. No doubt the person feels shut off by the quick negative reactions. Second, you ask the objectors why they are instantly resistant. Make them support their "won't work" statements. It's very easy to say "no" in a group without having to justify that response. Don't let objectors get away with it. Third, find out from other members how they feel about what has been said by both sides. In short, open the matter up to the entire group. Your knee-jerk resisters will begin to understand that simple resistance is not permissible behavior.

26. When people interrupt, let them know they are doing so. After a short time of being reminded and stopped, they'll understand that in your meetings, people have a chance to be fully heard.

27. Sometimes an idea will surface, then be ignored by everyone. It's almost as if they refuse to see what has surfaced. At that point, or after more discussion, come back to the contribution that was ignored and say, "I want to know what you think about what Carl said. Nobody responded at the time." You accomplish two ends: (1) You encourage Carl to continue to speak up; and (2) you insist on dealing with an issue

that might be valuable and certainly has been bypassed.

28. There's a fairly simple remedy for misunderstanding. Ask a listener to repeat what he or she heard the speaker say, before letting the listener respond further to the supposed meaning. If the listener is on target, let him or her proceed. If the listener is not, the speaker has a chance to clarify the meaning before discussion ensues.

29. No one should ever be successful in putting down another member of the group. Such behavior should be stopped immediately. You can break in to say, "I don't think it's appropriate to put anyone down. Stick with characterizing issues, and not people." If the offender says, "I didn't mean to do that," you can respond, "I'm telling you what I heard." You will probably not have to do more than that to discourage repetition.

Some of the preceeding problems and recommended steps are dealt with more fully in the accompanying sections.

Planning

A few planning steps taken before the meeting convenes can increase the effectiveness of that meeting. For example:

● **Announce your meeting sufficiently in advance so that people can prepare.** Outline the nature of the problem or the issue to be decided so that those who will attend can think through their ideas before the group meets. Participants will begin to build momentum before convening, so that meetings will get off the ground faster.

Tell people how to prepare—such as gathering information or developing questions. Research has shown that groups are better at evaluating ideas than at generating them, although proponents of brainstorming might disagree. One thing is sure: Brainstorming takes time. Let your people do at least some of that brainstorming in advance.

Allow time at the start of the meeting to go around the room and ask people for their ideas. Record each of the ideas and take no evaluations from others. People need to have a chance to air their contributions without fear of being cut-off or shot down. The only comments you'll take from others at this point are questions of clarification. You'll often find that excitement will begin to build during this exercise as people see the fruits of their thinking on paper. And since you're committed to sharing your leadership and creating a functioning work group, you'll benefit from the round robin, because everyone in the meeting is an equal.

• **Define the issue loosely.** Suppose you are up against a strong competitor in the Midwest who is able to sell at lower prices than you can. You might be tempted to define the problem as "How can we be more competitive in the Midwest?" By defining the issue that way, you have precluded certain solutions, for example, withdrawing from that market. It's preferable to define the issue in sufficiently broad terms so that you don't inhibit some creative solutions. Try posing the question this way: "We are not competitive in the Midwest. What should and can we do about it?"

• **Keep the group size proportionate to the purpose.** A smaller group is more conducive to interactions that make for good problem-solving. A larger group will be less interactive. Large groups can handle the transmission of information, al-

though there will be less participation.

• **Set a time limit.** Participants tend to be more comfortable knowing there will be closure by the end of a time period. If they walk into a conference room not knowing when they will emerge, they may actually experience tension and anger. They won't know how to establish their schedules around an open-ended meeting. You don't want your conferees dreading the meeting; you want them excited by it if possible.

Many people experience a dip in energy immediately after lunch. Midmorning is usually a better time for a stimulating meeting. Your "morning" people are still high in energy, and those who wake up slowly are on the up-curve. Meetings that start at, say, 10:30 in the morning, can capture both groups and give everyone a chance to settle into the day's routine, take care of urgent matters, the mail, and the rest of the day's schedule before disappearing into the conference room. People also know that the chances are good they'll be out around noon. The second preferred time for scheduling is midafternoon, when most people experience renewed energy.

People tend to operate more efficiently with a time limit, keeping their comments to a reasonable length, assuming the responsibility for timekeeping themselves.

Direct or Formal Leadership

As chairperson, you are charged with performing certain leadership roles that, at least at the beginning of a meeting, you can do best. As the meeting progresses, and the group becomes more effective and confident, others in the meeting may perform some of the direct, formal leadership roles. You'll want to encourage them to do so. Usually the most productive group is one in which the leadership is shared by many of the members. It's a sign that people are taking responsibility and "ownership" for what is happening.

Generally, people will assume leadership when the group is dealing with areas in which they have expertise and experience, or when they have strong opinions, or want to influence the group to consider certain issues or move in a specific direction.

Here are nine direct, formal roles you can perform as chairperson to get optimum results from your meetings:

1. State the problem. Presumably, you've already stated the problem as part of your planning. Do it again, since some of your subordinates may have developed different ways of stating the issue. Open the door for them to tell the group how they see what should be discussed. At this stage, you should make sure that everyone in the room understands the purpose and scope of the discussion. You may find that you have to provide some elaboration, some history, for some members of the group. Take the time now to do it. If you don't, you risk reducing their effectiveness because they have to catch up with the group. And until they do, they won't function well.

Add to your statement of the issue whatever information is necessary for a good solution to be found to decision to be made—resources, limitations, constraints, etc. You don't want to place too many restrictions on the group's work, of course, but you also don't want valuable time wasted while they generate ideas that, because of the law, policy of the organization, etc., can't possibly be applied to the problem.

If the group has a long-term task or objective, the current problem or issue should be stated in such a way that it can be seen in the long-range perspective.

2. Clarify the problem. The problem usually has to be restated from time to time during the meeting. One reason why is that problems have a way of changing their shape during scrutiny. The issue may become broader or narrower in scope than you believed originally. For example, you may discover that the competitive disadvantage in the Midwest is beginning to show itself elsewhere in the country. Or it might emerge that the product's life cycle is declining, and that a new product in the testing stage will or should replace the other.

3. Develop alternatives. Groups often tend to select one solution early in their discussions and ride with it to the exclusion of other solutions. (Later, when that solution shows flaws, you'll have to call another meeting and repeat the process.) It's your job to ensure that no possible option is excluded from the deliberation. No participants should go along with a proposed solution simply because they hesitate to express disagreement or reservations. Let those members who look hesitant, or are quiet, know that you value their opinions even if they dissent from the prevailing opinion in the group. At the same time, slow down the impatient associates who want to move quickly to a vote. Keep the discussion going until you and everyone else believes that all options and suggestions have been brought out. It takes longer to do that, but it cuts down on problems later.

4. Keep the discussion on the track. You can't afford to let the meeting wander all over the place unless you have a brainstorming session with no censuring. When the subject goes off the track, participants become bored, irritated, and uninvolved. Give a speaker enough time to get the essentials out before you take action to cut him or her off. You may not want to make the decision as to the speaker's relevance by yourself. A useful technique is to ask the speaker to relate what he or she is saying to the issue on the table. If the contributor doesn't convince you as to the relevancy, turn to the other members of the group and ask them whether they agree with you that the discussion has wandered. Be prepared to accept their decisions. They might have a different perception of the speaker's relevancy.

Keeping the discussion on the track is a difficult leadership role. You want to provide room and time for people to come up with imaginative ideas. At the same time, you don't want to turn others off with a boring, unproductive meeting. Bear in mind that one of the most common censorship ploys in a meeting is to declare, "I think we're getting off the subject." It's an effective way to avoid hearing what you do not want to hear. As the chairperson, you must take care not to impose censorship, and you must also make sure that others in the group don't. When the possibility arises, make it a group issue: Do others agree? What do others think?

5. Summarize. Sometimes the flow of ideas is so plentiful that members of the group lose sight of where they've gotten to. Or a fierce conflict develops in which the two sides refuse to budge from their seemingly divergent positions. At such moments, it's helpful to say something such as, "It seems to me that this is a fair summary of what's been said so far." Then, read from your notes and cover the main points

or positions. Your intervention gives everyone breathing space. It helps to highlight the various positions and define issues of any conflict. Incidentally, the disputants may find that they are not so far apart as they thought. Finally, a periodic summary can give participants a sense that they are, despite all of the opinions and dissents, making some progress toward the goal.

6. Define the consequences of the group's tentative choice. It's time to make sure that members understand what could or will happen if their tentative decision is carried out. What will the likely consequences be? Suppose the group believes it would be best to pull out of the Midwestern market and concentrate on other regions. What will that do to the profit picture? Could it affect long-range plans? What would be the impact on employees and on the marketing network in the Midwest? How would the action affect the image of the company? Try to discuss all possible effects, direct and indirect, now and in the future, negative *and* positive.

7. Test members' commitment to the decision. Now that they've considered the consequences, how involved and responsible do they feel about the proposed solution or decision? This is the last time for any member to express reservations or a hesitation that could create problems later. Resist any subtle pressure to move the group to adjournment if you suspect that there may still be some second thoughts. It's essential that each member is willing to assume responsibility and will be available to help implement the proposal if necessary.

8. Make the decision. Push for a firm statement that reflects the thoughts and feelings of the people around the table. Ask everyone whether he or she subscribes to the statement. To be absolutely sure there is agreement, you might call on members of the group to recite, in their words, what they have agreed to.

9. Create a plan of action. Once the decision has been made and agreed to, plan the implementation. Get further agreement on who does what, when, where, and how, with clear responsibilities outlined. You may wish to follow up the deliberations with a written summary so that it becomes extremely unlikely that any member of the group will be confused or uncertain about what has happened.

Informal, Indirect Leadership

In addition to your role as formal leader of the group, you have two others that are essential in building an effective, responsible work group that can benefit from participation: One role is to encourage the assumption of leadership roles by your subordinates; the other is to provide them with a model in the exercise of leadership in a group. The exercises of the leadership function include any of the preceding formal roles and the following constructive behaviors that everyone in your work group should practice:

• **Mediating.** Two people dispute each other's views. Very likely, if the dispute is intense or has been going on for a time, they are no longer listening to each other and are certainly not responding to each other. They have probably polarized, and they'd be capable of maintaining their stances indefinitely, with no forward movement. In mediation you intervene, not to arbitrate, but to illuminate. Ask each person to permit you to try to interpret his or her position as best you can in order for you, and the group, to understand that position better. After your interpretation, which should be as detached and objective as possible, ask each disputant to correct or add to what you have just said. By differentiating and clarifying their respective positions, you make it possible for everyone else to discuss each of the arguments sensibly. Then ask the group to do so, taking the arena away from the two members temporarily. It's important to restore some forward movement and progress to the group, which probably has been stalled for a time.

• **Harmonizing.** A similar situation exists: Two people in their debating have gone beyond the point at which they can effectively respond to each other. Chances are they are more interested in scoring debating points. Show them their areas of agreement or near-agreement. Suggest that they concentrate, for the moment, on building on the positive aspects rather than on their disagreement. Ask the group to help them in this effort. It is rare, even in the most intense conflict, that you cannot find some areas of agreement or potential agreement that the disputants are less capable of seeing.

• **Supporting.** She sits there quietly, but every so often she tries to get her words out, unsuccessfully. The tide of discussion sweeps past her. At the first opening, you say, "Martha's been trying to get her idea on the table, and I'd like to hear it. Let's give her a chance to tell us what she's thinking." John has actually voiced his idea, but he, too, has been totally ignored. Each time he finished, the discussion went on as if he had not said anything. You might say, "I'd like to have some chance to respond to John's idea, and I'd like to hear what the rest of you think about it. John, would you repeat what you said a few minutes ago?"

Supporting doesn't always require that you agree with the positions being expressed, but sometimes it means that you do: "That idea of yours, John, is very interesting. I think it has a lot of merit. Let's talk about it."

- **Gatekeeping.** Some of the members monopolize the discussion, making it very difficult for others to contribute. In effect, they have closed the gate. Now you open it. For example, you say, "I've heard you express your positions rather fully. I'd like to give some of the others a chance to express themselves." Then, look around the table for indications that someone wants to speak up, and give that person the nod. Or be even more forthright: "Jerry, you look as if you have something on your mind. If so, I'd like to hear it."

- **Listening.** It's safe to say that most people don't listen very well, especially if they're hearing something that, in some way, is unpleasant or threatening. Also, people in a group setting can get so absorbed in their own agendas that they cease to listen to what others may be saying. After you've listened to what Sheila has been saying, you hear Peter respond to her, but it seems to you that what Peter is saying does not relate closely to what you heard her say. You intervene with, "That's not what I thought Sheila said. Am I right, Sheila?" If you are correct, Sheila will agree, at which point you can suggest she repeat what she said. You've struck a blow for listening, and for accuracy. Listening is a vital role for everyone to play; it helps the group avoid talking at cross-purposes.

- **Confronting.** Both issues and people can get buried. When it happens, the group may sidestep views that it must consider because those views are painful. An example of a person getting buried: Jane has just made a suggestion that the group reconsider a point that had been discussed and discarded earlier. It is hard to know, from the way Jane expresses the suggestion, whether she understood the group's action. Tom replies sarcastically, "Jane proves there's always somebody who doesn't get the message. We took care of that ten minutes ago. Were you daydreaming about lunch?" A few people snicker. You intervene: "I think Jane has a right to say what she wants without having any of us embarrass her. Jane, why do you want us to reconsider that point?" You have properly chastised Tom for his treatment of Jane, which, if you had not intervened, could have had the effect of silencing her. And, you have opened the door for her to explain her suggestion.

Ideas and issues get buried too. Ralph contributes an idea to which Mike responds, "We tried that a few years back, and it was a disaster." So much for Ralph's thinking. But you say, "Wait a minute. I want to hear more about what Ralph is thinking, and I'd also like to know why Ralph thinks it might work better today than it did then."

When a group seems to sidestep an issue, or when members of the group behave in an aggressive or destructive manner toward others, confronting is a possible antidote. If you confront, stick to the behavior you observed or describe the impact of what you saw and heard on you. For example, "I'm puzzled — Sam brought up the X-12 product line and our disastrous service experience on it. It seems to me that we just ignored what he said. We went right on talking about something else." Or, "Maybe you weren't being sarcastic, Tom, but it sure sounded to me as if you were." No one can tell you that your perceptions were wrong. You, after all, are the expert on how you perceived what you saw and heard. They can only tell you that they differed in their perceptions. But at least you confronted the behavior or the issue.

Other Group-Building Functions

Here are some other approaches to building a group that works well in solving problems, generating ideas, and making decisions:

- **Discuss ideas with the whole group.** Prudy suggests an idea. Fred asks her a question about it. Then Myra tells Prudy what aspects of the idea she can't agree with. Jan says to Prudy that her idea is attractive, but it probably wouldn't work in the context the group is considering. Three exchanges, and Prudy is involved with all three. Does she feel pressure? If she's human, she does.

Have a rule that, once an idea is on the table, people must discuss it with the group as a whole. If the originator wants to talk too, fine. But he or she won't feel compelled to if not addressed personally. Group discussion takes the individual off the spot and creates the probability that others will enlarge and improve on the original. You'll also see your group saving time because a thoroughly defensive member doesn't feel he or she has to take up a lot of time defending the idea from perceived criticism.

- **Ask critics to be positive.** A member responds to another member's suggestion with, "That wouldn't work." You say, "Okay, what do you think has to be done with the idea to make it work?" Or, "What would you suggest as a work-

able idea?" The message you convey with your questions is "What you think might work is more helpful than what you think might not work." It's much easier to be negative than positive in a group. You don't, of course, want to completely eliminate negative responses, but you do want to encourage people to think of working with one another rather than shooting them down. Reward the positive and not the negative. (More about the nay-saying role later.)

A variation of the preceding technique: Under each idea put two columns marked "pro" and "con." When a person suggests a reservation, write it down in the "con" space, then ask the critic to suggest something for the "pro" space. If you follow that procedure regularly, you'll encourage people to see an idea as something to be evaluated as a whole.

- **Create group issues.** In one group that met on a continuing basis, one member's solution was adopted by the group over the dissent of another member. In a subsequent meeting, the dissenter severely criticized the colleague who had originated the idea. Other members sat in silence while the originator tried to defend herself and her idea. Eventually the chairperson stepped in by saying, "I'm wondering why we are letting Donna take all the heat for a decision the rest of us approved and agreed to. I think we should explain the action we took as a group. Donna doesn't have to be our spokesperson." Whereupon other members justified the decision and ultimately silenced the dissenter.

Don't let a member of the group become isolated. Few things will cause a work group to unravel more quickly than letting one member believe the group is against him or her or doesn't support the person, who feels exiled. And don't let one member of the group bear responsibility for what the whole group did or should have done.

• **Processing-observing.** There are three aspects of a group's work. One is the subject matter to be discussed, or the content. A second is the methodology, how it is to be discussed. The round-robin technique is an example of methodology, as is brainstorming. A third aspect of group problem-solving or decision-making is the process, which is what goes on between the members of the group—the group dynamics. Process is the aspect that is least dealt with by most groups. There are a lot of undercurrents, behaviors, power moves, control issues, that are not observed or understood. Unfortunately, these phenomena will often get in the way of a group's effectiveness. When a group has problems discussing issues, when personalities keep getting in the way, when certain subgroups are trying to get control, when other subgroups or individuals seem to be undermining the effectiveness of "rivals," these facts —or symptoms—should be recognized. Many times, the group is not aware of the dynamics because they are so immersed in the task. A process-observer might make comments such as, "In the past half hour, two proposals have been offered, and we don't seem to be able to deal with either one. We keep sliding away, and I think we'd better look at why we can't seem to deal with them," or, "I'm feeling frustrated because no one finishes a statement. Everyone is interrupting everyone else, and I don't know what we're talking about"; or, "I wonder why we keep talking about what happened at the Christmas party instead of our agenda."

Anything that seems to interfere with the group's getting on with its business is a matter for processing. The process-observer, whoever it might be, forces the group to look at itself while functioning, something that the group might not have done otherwise. Processing usually requires the group member to "step outside" the group's activities for a time to observe the dynamics.

Processing is not only a negative function. Sometimes the group works with great effectiveness, and that is legitimate subject matter for the processing. After all, the group needs to know what it does well just as much as what it does poorly, so that the effectiveness can be repeated.

Arriving at a Consensus

Many managers are not accustomed to working toward consensus decisions, which take time and patience. The payoff is usually a decision of higher quality than one arrived at by majority vote and there is a greater commitment to its implementation by members of the group. Here are some suggestions to follow:

1. Encourage all participants to have a full say. Create an atmosphere in which your subordinates feel free to voice even their slightest concerns or reservations. They won't do that if they are cut off by others or are made to feel that their concerns aren't worth anything. Make sure no one gets put down or shut out. In the first stages of the discussion, you may want to discourage debate so everyone can have his or her say. Accept the fact that people are genuinely concerned about what they express, and respect contributions even though you don't agree with them or believe they are very important.

People will soon express what is on their minds if they know they will not be belittled or besieged.

2. Emphasize positives. As noted, participants often are happier talking about what they dislike about a proposal than about what they think will work. Sum up, from time to time, what the people around the table think is good or will work. "You all seem to agree that this is going to involve an initial outlay of $25,000, but that it should be paying its way after about six months, maybe even making a profit."

3. Find out how serious the negatives are. One person in the group expresses reservations about a proposed change in procedure. You summarize what you understand the reservation to be and ask just how seriously the other person regards the problem. Or you may suggest ways to get around the problem and ask whether the member's reservations are still strong after listening to your alternatives: "Walter, if we were to create a new section to do that, would that take care of your problem?"

Sometimes, people value the chance to express their reservations even though they don't regard them as insuperable barriers. Too, they may feel, in the spirit of consensus, that they have an obligation to bring up any possible negative, no matter how minor. When they find that others don't share their fears, they let go of them. Once people start thinking in a positive way, they will often come up with suggestions on their own about how the problems they've defined can be solved.

4. Keep summing up the areas of agreement. With sufficient discussion and a clear respect within the group for everyone's contributions, you can expect the areas of agreement to widen. It isn't uncommon for a member who has been in disagreement with others to say something such as, "On second thought, I've seen it work at another company. Maybe it will work here, after all." Eventually, you may come to a point where problems and disagreements seem almost to melt away. This comes at the stage when people begin to realize that they are approaching a decision that will be acceptable to all, that the group is working together to remove all remaining obstacles. Consensus may then emerge quite suddenly.

Group Obstructive Behaviors

Just as there are behaviors that build effectiveness in a group, there are behaviors that get in the way of proper functioning of the group. As you read their descriptions, you'll recognize that you have seen such behaviors in many meetings you have attended. They are very common, so much so that people hardly think about them. Yet, they are destructive. Discourage them. Identify them for your subordinates. Make it very difficult for such behaviors to be successful for those who are responsible for them.

● **Shutting off.** One member silences another. There are many ways to do this. Perhaps the most usual shutting off technique is simply interrupting. Ann is in the midst of making a statement when Carl breaks in as if Ann were not talking. Sometimes the interruption is along the same line of thinking and, therefore, gets overlooked as a destructive behavior. It's even worse when Carl's remarks are unrelated. That would indicate that Carl was either not listening to Ann or that he regarded Ann's contribution as unimportant. When there is considerable interruption in a meeting, the indication is that the group members are not paying much attention to one another and/or are competitive. It's not likely that you'll get good decision-making from such a group.

Some people use humor to shut others off. Humor is especially effective in silencing people, probably because it is admired by many. A good sense of humor is considered an asset. Yet, humor can be used to humiliate. Ray, a former teacher, objects to what he considers to be a nonproductive debate between two other employees at a meeting he is attending. A fourth member of the group teases Ray: "The children are misbehaving. Teacher says." The barb, at which some people around the table laugh, destroys Ray's ability to get the meeting back on the track. In a similar situation, Ray's intervention might have encountered a psychological response from a group member who knew just enough about group dynamics to be obstructive: "Ray, you seem uncomfortable with any sort of disagreement, and you're always trying to smooth things over." Poor old Ray, he doesn't like any unpleasantness. His usefulness is destroyed.

Whatever the technique, shutting off tends to undermine a person's effectiveness. And he or she may actually withdraw from the group. The withdrawn person sits quietly, not about to risk further hurt.

Sometimes efforts to shut someone off produce fireworks. Sam says to Paula, "I don't think you understand the situation." That's an interruption that can be translated as, "You don't know what you're talking about." Paula protests that indeed she does. You can easily figure out where that interchange will go.

As leader, you must step in quickly to repair the damage when one subordinate shuts another off. Point out that the first person has been pre- vented from saying what he or she wants to say, that you would like to hear the rest. But in the case of more offensive behavior in which humiliation is involved, you can say, "I don't think it's necessary to embarrass Ray to make a point. Certainly I was embarrassed, even if Ray was not." Ask Ray to elaborate on his protest over the wrangling. Where the result of shutting off is anger, you can intervene with, "I'm not interested in making Paula prove she's an expert. I just want to hear what she has to say."

Eventually, your interrupters will get the message: The boss does not like people shutting others off. And others in the group, who are also annoyed by the technique, will follow your model.

• **Evaluating and analyzing.** You'll recall that Ray was "analyzed" in the preceding section: He was told that he gets uncomfortable when people disagree and tries to silence conflict. Another person, who seriously questions a premise that others in the group accept, receives the label of "negative."

When people in a group evaluate others, they put labels on the others' behavior. When they analyze, they suggest attitudes and motivations. For example, when someone responds to another with some heat, then the latter says, "I don't know why you're so defensive." Or, "Why are you so angry?" The list goes on and on. "I really think you're projecting." "You seem to get very uptight every time we bring up the subject of the . . ." "Just because you didn't get your way on the scheduling matter, you . . ."

In an effective group, people talk about their perceptions of others, or how the behavior of others affects them. For example: "I'm sorry if I have made you angry"; or, "You seem upset by what I just said. Am I right?" The perceiver is an expert in his or her perceptions. No one can tell you how you feel. They can, however, reply that your view of the situation is not the same as theirs. Fine. No more argument. But if someone tells you that you are angry or tense, you may say that is not true. Then, the two of you can argue, indefinitely, about whether you are or not.

Thus, when you hear members of your group labeling others or analyzing their motives, insist that they talk in terms of their perceptions on how the behavior of others affects them. This will get the message across without offending or inviting a backlash. "I'm very distressed that you seem to believe I missed those deadlines because I didn't care." "I didn't say that." "I'm just telling you what I thought you said."

● **Dominating.** People who try to take over a meeting may not even be aware of what they are really doing. The would-be dominator may rationalize, "Well, I'm a person who likes to get things done. Let's cut through all this garbage and get this settled." Unfortunately, many dominators regard everything that doesn't conform to their views as garbage. The dominator wants influence, and often goes after it in a heavy-handed way. Sometimes he will try to determine the course of a meeting at the outset. Other times, he will wait until conflict or stalemate develops, then move in. Frequently the dominator will make a strong case, gather a few allies, then push for a quick vote.

If shared leadership is so desirable, what's wrong with having strong-minded people in your meetings who know what they want and move quickly to get it? The answer is that the dominator is less concerned about the well-being and objectives of the group than for his or her personal agenda—and will usually think nothing of subverting the group's progress toward its goals to achieve his or her own. There's nothing wrong with a conference room full of people with their own agendas, so long as they agree that the product of the group's work should be what is best for the group. The dominator probably does not subscribe to that good intention.

When you are confronted by a person who out-talks everyone else, seems impatient with listening to others, interrupts frequently, tries to trample over opposition, and obviously wants to ram his or her agenda through, you must take action—and show others how to neutralize the worst effects of the dominator. You don't want to shut the dominator off completely, because the person has leadership abilities that could help the group if channeled properly.

Some **don'ts** in handling this kind of person: Don't turn the meeting into an arena between the dominator and you. He or she will probably enjoy the performance, but little else will get done. Don't remain silent while the dominator tries to build his or her influence. Both the dominator and others will see that as acquiescence.

On the positive side, get the group involved. Instead of engaging head to head with the dominator, direct your remarks to the group and encourage them to talk. If you can't get them to respond to your comments, ask questions. When the dominator pushes for early votes, say, "I don't think we're ready to close this out. I'm sure we could come up with some more points."

You don't want to destroy the dominator. You do, however, want to dilute some of his or her obstructive behavior.

• **Nay-saying.** Negative responses have great impact in meetings. It's always easier to turn an idea down than to take the time and trouble to give it the consideration it deserves. Some people achieve prominence in a meeting through their continually playing devil's advocate. Others prefer not to take risks, and a "no" eliminates the risk.

Some steps to counter negativism have already been described earlier in this chapter. Much of the impact of the nay-saying, indeed much of the nay-saying itself, will fade as you make the group comfortable with itself and make its members supportive of one another. In addition, clarify any risks. No one wants to be taxed with making a mistake. But in some cases, you can point out, a mistake is less deadly than in others. Certain decisions will not bankrupt the company. In fact, you might consistently encourage the group to answer the question, "What's the worst that can happen if we choose this option?" If the stakes are not as high as people first imagine, the consequences of not making a decision could be worse for all concerned.

You can confront the negative behavior more straightforwardly, if you like, by asking such questions as, "Why the pressure to hold off?" or, "How do the dangers outweigh the possible benefits?" or "Look, I think you are closing out chances to consider this fairly."

• **Conveying negative signals.** This section probably applies to you as manager more than to anyone else. Until you develop a group that can operate as a confident entity, you'll find that members of your group will be dependent on you for many of their reactions and evaluations. They'll frequently look for clues from you as to how they should regard others in the group, as well as their ideas. Therefore, be conscious of the following signals:

Facial expressions. You may not agree with what is being said or believe it is of very high quality. And you may reflect your opinions on your face. You may even be thinking of something quite unrelated that is not pleasant, and your face reflects your displeasure. Try to keep your face from registering any negative emotions; otherwise people will feel that you are discounting the importance of what is being said.

Show of impatience. Managers shuffle papers, fidget, glance at their watches, while someone else is talking. It seems as if they are saying, "The speaker is not very important. I wish he'd hurry up." Or immediately after the other person has finished speaking, the manager starts to talk about something quite different, as if to say, "Forget what he just said. It doesn't count."

Talking through. You have something on your mind that you'd like to clear up immediately, even though someone else has the floor. You lean over and ask a question, or start a conversation with a neighbor. Others will wonder what you are saying and won't bother to concentrate on the speaker. You're also suggesting that the speaker is not worth your listening to.

How a Group Develops

There are stages in the development

of a group, whether that group be a work group, a task force, quality circle, etc. Being able to recognize these developmental stages can help you to provide constructive leadership that can result in further development. Not recognizing the steps of group growth can lead to frustration, dissension, obstructive behavior by its members, even to failure of the group in its task.

1. The initial phase in the operation of a new group is often characterized by confusion over the roles to be played by the members, the task to be performed, the type of leadership, and where it is to come from. People may have been assigned to the group, but they do not yet perceive themselves to be part of it. The group is still a collection of individuals.

This is a searching phase: "What are we here for?" "What part shall I play?" "What am I supposed to do?" "Why were these others designated?" "Who is the leader?" "What are his or her qualifications?" "Who is going to tell us what we are supposed to do?"

With the confusion, you can also expect to find anxiety, even anger, and, certainly, dependency. When roles and tasks are unclear, people will experience anxious feelings. They may be angry because they have been thrust into a new situation without knowing how to deal with it. Even though you are committed to participative management, you cannot expect the new group members to be self-sufficient. They need leadership. They are dependent on you. You must respond to that need. Give them a sense of direction and structure.

In this searching stage, much of what goes on between people is ostensibly centered on the task to be performed by the group. The interactions will reflect biases, preconceptions, and antagonisms brought in from the outside. The roles that people choose for themselves will often resemble those they have in their work situations.

2. The second stage involves a definition of the task to be performed or the objective to be reached by the group. People begin to see themselves and the role they play in relation to the task or objective. They are not yet a group, rather they are an aggregate of people who have a common task.

Identifiable interactions emerge. Often conflicts occur between those members who want to get the task done quickly and those who want to proceed more deliberately. Or, between those who have a firm idea of how the task should be performed and those who prefer to experiment. Some people will insist on applying solutions they have brought with them, while others will worry about whether the task has been defined correctly and realistically. There will be members who want a strong, autocratic direction and others who would like to see a more democratic, open atmosphere maintained.

There are many personal agendas to be recognized. Some members want to gain influence in the group, either because they see themselves as leaders or because they have their own tasks they would like to see the group perform. Others want to use the group to gain publicity and visibility for themselves. Still others might wish to create an informal group in opposition to formal management.

Some of the personal agendas will be obvious and will be confronted—or ignored—by the group. If they are not resolved, they will probably show up later. What often happens is that task-oriented leadership will emerge to get the group moving toward its objective. Processing and attention to the group dynamics will probably be discouraged. Those sorts of things will be seen as barriers to progress. Ironically, people who assume the task-oriented leadership now may be discarded later, even resented, because of their insensitivity to the people issues that invariably arise in a group.

3. The group now begins to approach coalescence. Members may sense that they are no longer a collection of individuals, but that their behavior is influenced by membership in this group and by interaction with other members. They will begin to define for themselves group roles that are different from the individual roles they brought in, or that they played in the initial stage. These roles generally revolve around facilitating and servicing the group toward its objective. There is a strong commitment to that objective. Attention is also given to group process, because people in the group want it and its members to be effective. There is a realization that unresolved conflicts and personal issues (or agendas) not confronted can obstruct the progress of the group. However, some personal agendas involving influence, achievement, esteem, visibility and leadership are now compatible with the group's mission. Indeed, those agendas are often worked out in the group roles people select for themselves.

Up to the point of coalescence, the group was fragmented. Either each member retained individuality or joined with subgroups looking for power. Now the fragmentation fades as the group takes on a personality of its own.

4. Groups that continue for a period of time, that are engaged in complex tasks, move considerably beyond the coalescence phase. They no longer concern themselves only with getting the task done; they seek ways in which to be more effective in getting it done. They learn. They also begin to learn how they learn. They become self-evaluative as a means of increasing their expertise.

Groups that were formed to perform definite, finite tasks usually die when they have achieved their objective. In your department, you will often see groups die and reform into other groups. The key is to continue to provide these groups with new tasks and opportunities for achievement.

Evaluating Your Meetings

Your meetings provide excellent opportunities for you to build your work group(s) and to share your leadership. You might want to consider placing some of the responsibility for this effective group development on the people who are your subordinates and members of the group. Their reward is, among other things, getting more of the results they'd like from their efforts.

One way to enhance their group skills is to encourage them to evaluate their performance individually and as a group. After each meeting, distribute an evaluation form to each participant. A sample form follows. You can transcribe the information to a master sheet or to a graph that shows how the members of the group feel about their effectiveness. Or you may decide simply to let each person keep his or her evaluation private. Whether you go public with the information or not depends on how much risk you and the others believe the work group can absorb.

There is always some risk in going public with personal evaluations. But there is a payoff. After the initial hesitation in sharing evaluations of self and others, there is satisfaction and a sense of achievement in members' abilities to work well with one another. Thus there is visible progress, and that constitutes reinforce-ment and encouragement. The progress is likely to continue until you have a work group that can be open, supportive, collaborative; that confronts issues directly and promotes group objectives. For you, perhaps most important of all, the group becomes a powerful resource.

Here is a sample evaluation form that you may wish to adapt for your meetings:

1. How effective was the meeting?
   Explanation: Did people commit themselves to work for what they perceived to be the best interests and most realistic objectives of the group? Were the resources of the group efficiently applied to achieve those objectives? Do you believe that the group's achievement was the best that could be hoped for?

10	9	8	7	6	5	4	3	2	1

   Most effective   Somewhat effective   Ineffective

2. How clear were the group's goals in this meeting?

10	9	8	7	6	5	4	3	2	1

   Quite clear   Somewhat clear   Unclear

3. To what extent did we stay on track in working toward the group's objectives and avoiding distractions?

10	9	8	7	6	5	4	3	2	1

   Completely on track   More on than off   Sidetracked

4. How would I judge my effectiveness in promoting the group's work?

10	9	8	7	6	5	4	3	2	1

   Very effective   Somewhat effective   Ineffective

5. To what extent did the group consider my contributions?

10	9	8	7	6	5	4	3	2	1

   Totally   Somewhat   Incompletely

6. How free did I feel to express my opinions and make contributions in the group?

10	9	8	7	6	5	4	3	2	1

   Totally   Guardedly   Not at all

7. Overall, what was my level of satisfaction with the meeting?

10   9   8   7   6   5   4   3   2   1

Well satisfied   Somewhat satisfied   Dissatisfied

8. How would I describe the atmosphere of the meeting (check applicable words):

_____ Avoiding issues	_____ Enjoyable
_____ Contentious	_____ Productive
_____ Nit-picking	_____ Collaborative
_____ Competitive	_____ Productive

Above is an example of the master sheet you might keep on your meetings to provide feedback for your subordinates. The individual ratings for each meeting are averaged and that average is noted above the session number. You may want to maintain a master sheet for each question you ask individuals to evaluate. For example, the clarity of group goals, level of satisfaction, etc. Or you may use different colors to represent each one on the master sheet.

It's possible that your ratings will start high, then dip before climbing again. The reason for this is that, initially, people tend to be very cau-

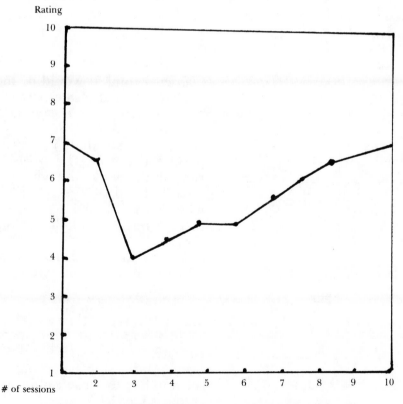

Figure 1   How Effective Are Our Meetings?

tious in their assessments of themselves and the group. It takes a certain amount of risk-taking ability to be able to say, "I don't think we were very effective after all." As the group members begin to take the meetings evaluations seriously, and develop confidence that they won't be "punished" for assessing the meetings honestly, the ratings will dip for a time.

Such a profile is not a universal phenomenon, a "law," but it is quite natural and explainable.

Identifying Group Roles

The following is a transcript of a meeting in which several employees are involved. As you read through it, identify in the spaces provided in the margins the role that an employee is playing at that point. The purpose of this exercise is to help reinforce in your mind the various constructive and obstructive roles people can play in groups. The roles to be identified are:

Constructive	Obstructive
Processing-observing	Dominating
Confronting	Evaluating and analyzing
Listening	Shutting off
Gatekeeping	Nay-saying
Supporting	
Mediating	
Harmonizing	
Summarizing	

Charles: I think it would be most practical to bring the salespeople into the home office for the introduction of the new X-12 line.

Ted: I can't see that. To have all those people roaming the halls and disrupting the work, and what's more—

Phyllis: Hold it, Ted. I'd like to hear why Charles thinks it's better to bring them here than to hold regional meetings.

Charles: I think it'll be less disruptive overall. In one week, we can accomplish what would take us five weeks to do on a regional basis.

Mark: We tried that on the Servus-all line, and it was a disaster. Why repeat it?

Larry: Mark, stop being negative. You seem to like to throw cold water on everyone's ideas.

Mark: I think that's uncalled for. I was in the middle of all that mess on Serv-

1. _____

2. _____

3. _____

4. _____

5. _____

6. _____

7. _____

8. _____

9. _____

usall. I'm talking from intimate experience.

Phyllis: Aside from the time element,
Charles, are there any other advantages
to making the introduction here?

Charles: Sure. All the top brass can be
available to give it a lot of pizzazz.
They may not be able to travel around
for five weeks. I'll bet Harry Brown
would be willing to give a speech. . . .

Mark: (Groans loudly)

Charles: What's wrong with that?

Mark: You want to send them out of
here charged up, not half-asleep.

Charles: He *is* chairman.

Phyllis: Sandra, you've been sitting
there awfully quiet. Do you want to say
something about all this?

Sandra: I'm wondering why it's so bad
to bring them in here and get it all over
with? Ted thinks it will be so disruptive. For whom?

Ted: Every time salespeople come in,
they've got all sorts of problems that
just have to be taken care of yesterday.
Just try to get some work done that
week with all of them demanding special attention.

Sandra: What's your alternative?

Ted: Have regional meetings. They're
smaller. You can spend more time with
individuals. You can probably accomplish everything in three days that it
would take five to do with a big group.

Charles: But that's overlooking something very important. You're going to
have at least a three-week lag between
introduction in one region and the last.

Mark: So what's the big deal about
three weeks or so?

Charles: I think it's very important.

Mark: It's nit-picking.

Phyllis: Hold it, you guys. I don't want
to sit here all morning listening to you
two fight. Let's take a look at where we
are. I'm going to use the flip chart. On
one side, Charles wants us to bring the
salespeople into the home office all at
once for a one-week meeting. What are
the advantages?

Charles: Saves time. One week instead of three, maybe four.

Sandra: We can get the top brass involved in kicking it off.

Phyllis: There's something else that Charles implied that we ought to think about. If we had a general meeting, everybody would go out there and start selling the new line at once.

Mark: I still don't see why we're making such a big deal about three weeks. It's almost nothing.

Phyllis: That's not true. If we have a national ad campaign, it'll break all at once. Some of our people won't be selling it for two or three weeks after. That could cost us a lot of business.

Sandra: Write that down, Phyl. Now what about Ted's points? And Mark's?

Phyllis: Okay. It's less disruptive to have regional meetings. Anything else?

Charles: I've finally figured out the real reason for Ted's wanting to have regional meetings. He wants to live off the expense account for all that time and travel around the country.

10. _____

Ted: Very funny. Do you know what long hours you have to spend when you're doing these meetings? I'm talking about eighteen-hour days.

Sandra: I'm still waiting for some more arguments from Ted or Mark.

Mark: Ted said we can spend more time with individuals in the smaller meetings. That's true, and I think it's important.

Ted: We're all missing a big point. Do you realize how much money we'd save in taking people out of the field for, say, three days instead of five?

11. _____

Sandra: Hey, I've got a great idea.

Phyllis: Wait a minute, Sandra. I think we ought to talk about Ted's point.

Charles: I don't think it's so significant. If you have the meetings during the week, you'll have travel time. That'll wipe out much of the savings.

12. _____

Mark: Now that really *is* nit-picking.

Larry: Mark, I guess when you don't

13. _____

14. _____

15. _____

16. _____
17. _____

18. _____

19. _____

20. _____

want us to consider an issue, you put it down. You groan as if someone is ridiculous, or you call people nit-pickers. I just want you to know that I don't think you're being helpful to the rest of us when you do that.

Mark: Well, **excuse me.**

Phyllis: I don't think any one us can boast that we've done a great job looking at all the options. There's a lot of anger that keeps getting in the way.

Charles: What do you mean, a lot? So far as I can see, only one of us has been showing anger. That's Mark.

Ted: I didn't much appreciate your crack about my wanting to travel and live off the company, Charles. I thought that was unnecessary.

Mark: My, we *are* getting touchy.

Larry: I don't think *I'm* touchy, but I don't think you've been a positive influence.

Sandra: You know, I think Mark was right about one thing. Harry Brown isn't a great speaker. We had him at a convention we held in Boca Raton, and he does tend to drone on. You know, really, one to one he's great. But when he gets up in front of a group, he puts everyone to sleep. What's the matter, Charles? You look as if you disagree with me.

Charles: I'm disagreeing with what you just did.

Sandra: I probably shouldn't talk about the chairman that way.

Charles: I don't mean that. Larry was onto something that has to be dealt with, Mark has been very sarcastic and almost nasty, I think. And just when Larry was forcing us to deal with it, you come up with something totally irrelevant.

Sandra: I just thought it was more important than throwing mud at each other. That doesn't help.

Larry: I'm not trying to throw mud on Mark. I just wanted him to know that I think he could be more helpful.

21. _____

22. _____

23. _____

24. _____

25. _____

26. _____

27. _____

Mark: I guess what I'm saying to you is that I think this meeting is a big waste of time.

Charles: You're doing your share to make it that way.

Phyllis: I don't think anybody here is really doing their full share to make this meeting productive. I wonder why we can't be more respectful even though we disagree? We seem to be more interested in cutting other people off than in really listening. Why can't we take time to list the pros and cons of each position and evaluate them?

Larry: Let me try something. Charles, as I understand it, you want to bring everyone in here for one week. That way, everyone gets the same start on the new line. And we can put on a better show here to kick it off, having the brass come in. Is that right?

Charles: Right. And don't forget the travel time. They'll come in on Sunday night or Monday morning, and they'll go home on Friday.

Larry: Okay. Ted, you and Mark seem to want regional meetings. You say it's too disruptive to have a couple hundred salespeople invading us. You also feel that the regional meetings would allow more one-to-one coaching. Am I right?

Ted: Yeah, and don't forget that each person would be out of the field for less time.

Phyllis: Sandra, you've been awfully quiet.

Sandra: I was told to shut up.

Ted: No, you weren't. You were interrupting me. Phyllis said we ought to consider my point first.

Phyllis: You said you had an idea.

Sandra: Let's send them all the printed material ahead of time. They can read it, then come to the meeting, and we could probably cut the meeting time to three days, from five. If we did that, we'd be able to have everyone in at the same time, without taking them out of the field for long.

Larry: Let me pick up on that. Ted's

worried that to have the meeting here would be disruptive. Okay. He also wants salespeople to have more individual attention. We'll break the meeting into two segments, have one in the East and the other in the West. We won't come near the home office. The first segment starts on Monday morning and goes till Wednesday. The second starts on Thursday and goes to Saturday. One group travels on Sunday, the other on Saturday. That ought to work out evenly and fairly.

28. _____

Charles: Yeah, and we'll get the brass committed to one week. That sounds like the best of both worlds.

Phyllis: I wonder if the salespeople will do the required reading?

Mark: No. And if they don't, three days is not long enough. I think we ought to break and take up this thing again tomorrow.

29. _____

Larry: They are grown-up people, Phyllis. They have to take responsibility. We can't spoon-feed them. Sandra, do you like the two-segments idea?

Sandra: Yes.

Larry: Phyllis?

Phyllis: To expedite things, we can break large segments into smaller groups. That'll speed up learning.

Mark: But you're still going to have one group coming into the home office?

Sandra: You didn't listen. Larry said that both groups would meet away from the home office.

30. _____

Larry: So does everyone agree? That's the way we'll do it. It's all settled.

Charles: I'm not sure. How do we know that if we boil it down to three days, we'll do a good job?

31. _____

Larry: We can. Don't worry about it.

Charles: I think we ought to write out a rough design just so we can be sure that three days is enough, with half the sales force.

Larry: Charles, if we do that now, we're going to be here 'til dinner. Let's vote on it now and work out the details later.

Answers to Identifying Group Roles

1. It's a mild shut-off, with a touch of nay-saying. Not serious.
2. Supporting
3. Nay-saying with a mild shut-off. Mark is trying to preclude further discussion.
4. Evaluating and analyzing
5. Supporting
6. A familiar shut-off by ridiculing
7. Gatekeeping
8. Shut-off
9. Summarizing
10. Evaluating and analyzing with hoped for shut-off consequences.
11. Shut-off
12. Shut-off
13. Confronting
14. Processing-observing
15. Confronting
16. Confronting
17. Shut-off
18. Confronting
19. Shut-off by switching to another, "safer" subject
20. Confronting with some processing-observing
21. Confronting and shut-off
22. Processing-observing
23. Supporting and summarizing
24. Supporting and summarizing
25. Gatekeeping
26. Listening
27. Harmonizing
28. Harmonizing
29. Nay-saying
30. Listening
31. Dominating. Larry has seized the advantage and is now trying to close out the discussion without any further questions or dissent.

Chapter Nine

Using Small Groups

While the small, problem-solving group is hardly unknown to our organizations, it's safe to say that most managers have not used them consistently and efficiently, and have certainly not realized the full spectrum of benefits that these small groups, such as committees, quality circles, and task forces, can produce. Of the three kinds of problem-solving groups, the task force is probably the most flexible. It can be used for decision-making, the introduction of change, the formation of new management groups or ventures, the enrichment of jobs, management development, and identification of managerial talent. It is a wide-ranging tool for the manager who is committed to leadership sharing, and a relatively safe tool for that purpose. Although most of this section can apply to the use of any kind of small groups, a number of recommendations will relate to the successful operation of the task force.

The ideal task force has the following characteristics: It is . . .

. . . *temporary*. It is formed to accomplish a task. It has temporary authority and responsibility. The task force has a natural life. When its task is completed, it "dies."

. . . *operational*. It has responsibility for what it proposes. Its work is not usually considered done until there are instruments or organizations created to carry out its work. If a task force is separated from the implementation of what it has recommended, it becomes, in effect, another committee, with advisory functions only.

. . . *interdepartmental* or *interfunctional*. The task force cuts across boundaries and functions. It is an instrument of collaboration.

. . . *interdisciplinary*. Its makeup may include chemists, engineers, financial specialists, marketing people. Many problems are multidimensional. No one discipline can contain all the knowledge necessary to make the best decisions.

... *semiautonomous*. The group should be free to establish its schedule, methods of operation, means of resolving the issue it is charged with considering, and perhaps even to determine its leadership. The task force members should be free from interference by their regular or functional managers. As manager, you should provide an umbrella of authority under which the task force functions.

Finally, within the ideal task force, decisions are made by consensus. Majority rule too often limits openness and commitment. The members of a task force should believe that whatever decision is made, whatever action is taken, is probably the best that could be achieved under the circumstances and is certainly superior to what any member could achieve on his or her own.

Task-Force Bonuses

In addition to the solution or decision generated by a successful task force, a number of benefits accrue to you, the manager, and to its members as a result of its work. For example, the task force can create a *management reservoir*. Such a small group can create very realistic criteria for management and supervisory selection. In the first place, the testing is done in genuine risk situations. The stakes are real, as could be the rewards, and the behavior is significant. In a simulation, a person may be encouraged to take more chances than he or she would in facing real risk. In a task-force situation, you can see how the group member handles the responsibility and risk, which are very real. At the same, for your sake, the risk is hardly

without limit. There are probably constraints on the operation of the task force that you have imposed, and the other members of the group provide limits and braking.

The task force provides a variety of evaluation possibilities. In addition to the employee's regular or functional manager, you can obtain assessments of the performance from the task-force leader and from its other members.

The task force goes a long way toward solving your problem of what to do with the employee who cannot, at least for the time being, be promoted, or who is unsuited to be promoted further, yet has much knowledge and skill to offer your department. Some managers have used task-force participation as a means of actually removing a manager from a job at which he or she is no longer effective.

Keep your management potential busy and challenged on task forces. They may not yet have the title they seek, but they are progressing. They enjoy authority beyond what they would possess outside the group. They are learning and acquiring new skills. And, if their task forces function as they should, the members have prestige and distinction within the organization.

One of the most serious problems a manager faces is that of the older subordinate who has retired on the job. He or she is a shelf-sitter, blocking the progress of others. Yet, this person has much experience and knowledge that are still valuable. Create a task force in which he can contribute that experience and knowledge, and move him or her out of the blocking position.

Another valuable benefit of the task force is in *training* and *learning*. Adults need reasons for learning. How well a person learns depends in large part on that person's expectation that his or her behavior will result in solving a problem or achieving a goal.

The problem with classroom learning, where much training takes place, is that the learner is often unable to see the reward for behaving in a certain way, simply because he or she is removed from the work environment where immediate feedback is available. For example, the learner is taught new management techniques in a classroom. The reward for applying such techniques will come back on the work scene. Since there is a passage of time between the learning and the applying, the person may not be strongly motivated to practice the new techniques.

A task force, on the other hand, with its almost simultaneous feedback and reinforcement of effective behavior, sets up a learning situation quite superior to what most classrooms can provide. The pragmatic, on-the-job education of the task force involves here-and-now risk. Members on the task force very quickly find out when they are effective with others, and when they are not. And the accomplishment of the goal provides a valuable reward for the learning.

Job enrichment is a significant benefit from the use of the small group, especially the task force. The point of job enrichment is to provide a challenge to the employee, to make the work more important and interesting, to keep the employee in a learning and growth situation, which, has strong motivational value. The task force is a good way of "loading" a person's job with more significant contents and more responsibility.

No doubt you have employees who are in an overlearning situation, and that fact can threaten your building

and maintaining an effective, highly motivated work group. You may be unwilling or unable to promote the employee in an overlearning situation. But the task force offers an alternative.

Thus the task force provides benefits beyond solving problems and making decisions that exceed the resources that any one department, function, or discipline can muster. Its value in assessing training and developing management, expanding talents that exist in potential, enriching jobs at all levels, and building collaboration, is inestimable.

Forming the Task Force

Who should sit on a task force? How large should it be? Are there jobs a task force shouldn't be asked to handle? These are questions that invariably arise in any consideration of a team approach to problem-solving and decision-making. There are few hard-and-fast guidelines, but here are some considerations:

Size. The size usually depends on what kind of a job is to be done, how many functions are involved, and how many kinds of expertise are needed. In most cases, eight, possibly up to ten, constitute a reasonable maximum. You want optimum interactions between participants. You must also consider the constraints of the number of schedules to be coordinated and the expense of taking people off their regular jobs.

There is, in making up a task force, a temptation to bring in as many resources as possible. But as the group becomes larger and harder to coalesce, the point of diminishing returns will be reached.

Membership. The best qualification for a member of a task force is that you think you cannot spare that person from his or her duties. Find a way to spare the employee, because he or she is probably a prime task-force candidate. If you have the best people, the task force will have proportionate prestige and importance in the eyes of others. You also want the best people to feel rewarded. The task force is a reward for their good performance. And you want the task force to work as well as possible, and for that you need the most knowledgeable people possible.

Try to get people who interact well. That doesn't mean homogeneity. Too many people in a group who think the same way can spell trouble for your task force. Mix people who have the following characterisics: They are . . .

. . . *analytical.* They have the ability to diagnose the causes of a problem, to pull pieces of a situation apart so that they can be examined more easily. These are the "why" people.

. . . *judgmental.* They evaluate, test, and measure the practicality of an idea and are able to foresee the direct and indirect consequences of its application.

. . . *creative.* People who think associatively are those we usually term creative. They see links and connections between ideas that other people simply don't see.

Types of tasks. There are at least two conditions under which a group can be expected to be less efficient than individuals:

1. When time is a factor and you must have an early decision. Short deadlines tend to keep the group from warming up properly, from opening up, from building the trust necessary for collaboration. The greatest dangers, in a pressure atmosphere, are that the leadership will become autocratic, or that the first solution that even sounds feasible,

will be adopted without sufficient evidence, or that the group will be so paralyzed by the time pressure that nothing will happen. Consensus is the strength of the task force approach, but it takes time to achieve it.

2. Problems that can best be solved by quantitative methods eliminate or severely reduce the opportunity for qualitative analysis and speculation.

Some areas that lend themselves to deliberation by a task force:

- Determining and designing effective training
- Reorganizations of work flow or departments
- Distribution channels
- Restructuring of a sales force
- Computerization
- Start-up of a new program, project, or product
- Resolution of causes of conflict
- Establishing new interdepartmental collaboration
- Merging of existing functions or departments
- Bettering service operations
- Eliminating barriers to productivity
- Introduction of new management systems or structure.

These are just a few of the areas in which your task force can operate effectively and provide an invaluable resource for you. You don't really have to look very far for issues on which your task forces can work. No doubt there are projects you've wanted to initiate or at least experiment with, but you just never had the time. Or there were flaws in the operation that, while not serious enough to constitute a firing an employee, have nagged at you. Or you said to yourself, "I know there are better ways to operate."

Autonomy. No task force can

operate with complete autonomy, but you can provide the authority necessary during its life for it to get its job done. Anticipate that a task force may have to redefine its objective, as it grapples with the issues, or to select a new one. In each case, the task force negotiates with you as to how much room it has to move in.

Your umbrella of authority also enables the group to work with people outside the task force—other employees, other managers, other departments. Your authority will also prevent or reduce the amount of interference members of the group might experience from others as they complete their tasks.

Leadership in a Task Force

The most obvious—and traditional —way to select a leader for your task force is to designate the person of highest authority. But the amount of a person's authority should not be the only criterion. Aside from technical and managerial qualifications, the leader should be experienced in process, with proven ability to function effectively as part of a group, and have as one personal goal the wish to help the group successfully accomplish its objectives.

The authority, power, and influence of the leader should have no internal significance for the task force. Often the less authority the leader tries to bring into the group, the better everyone performs.

In addition to selection by authority, there are at least four other ways to select a task force leader. One is to tap the person whose initiative and efforts have resulted in the formation of the group—the person who first defined the problem or brought the challenge to your attention. A second way is to choose the person who will be heading up a permanent group that will continue to implement what the task force resolves. A third criterion for selection derives from the operational area most involved in the tasks force's objective. For example, if the goal is a new product, even though research, engineering, finance, and sales are all involved, the group leader might well be a marketing manager.

The fourth method of selection is easily the most intriguing: Let the task force choose its own leader. At the same time, the group will usually let it be known what it expects of a leader: how formal the leadership should be, how much personal authority he or she is expected to wield, how firm or "loose" the style, etc.

The leader should perform the leadership roles described in the previous section on group development. But he or she also has certain vital roles to play outside the task-force meetings, roles that should be considered in selecting the person who will head the task force. For example:

• **Linking pin.** In a team-oriented organization, the task force leader will probably be a member of other teams or groups, and it is likely that some of the work that the task force does relates to tasks and responsibilities of others. It is the leader's job to establish and maintain collaboration between the related groups. Certainly, he or she is the link with you. If there is only the one task force operating, the leader maintains liaison with the regular, functional managers who are affected by his or her group's tasks.

• **Protector.** This is a traditional role of the manager, but one that, unfortunately, is often given short shrift. In the life of every task force, there will be intergroup conflicts: toes of those outside the task force will be stepped on and boundaries of other units will be crossed as the team pursues its objectives. Inevitably, there will be those who feel that the task force has been given too much authority, that its authority overlaps the jurisdiction of regular managers. The team leader, therefore, will have to smooth ruffled feathers, explain team functions to those who are not participating, and serve as a buffer. Whatever suspicion, complaints, or anger are aroused by the activities of his or her group, it is the leader who must bear the brunt. He or she must not permit the comments and actions of those outside the task force to impede its effectiveness. He must keep communications open between the task force and "outsiders," and, at the same time, insist that those communications be directed through him or her.

• **Clearinghouse for task-force operations.** Some of the work of the task force will be conducted between meetings, and the leader must ensure that all extra-meeting work be cleared by him or her. The leader should be apprised of all problems, progress, and needs that arise between sessions.

• **Negotiator and evaluator.** Con-flicts in schedules, priorities, and duties will arise. The leader will have to settle them through negotiations with the managers concerned. To add to your own knowledge, you may ask the leader to evaluate the effectiveness of the various members of the task force.

Perhaps the most important role of the leader, internally and externally, is to make sure that his or her leadership is shared by other members of the group. During the meetings, there must be opportunities for other members to assume temporarily dominant roles. These temporary roles enable a member to exercise expertise in the area under consideration at the moment. But there are other justifications for the temporary assumption of leadership—for example, a person's self-interest or the skills he or she possesses could enhance the group's deliberations at that point. Unless the leadership of the task force is available to be borrowed by other members, the chance is great that the resources of the group will be inadequately utilized.

Another reason why the formal leader must encourage others to take over the leadership role for periods of times is to offset that person's vested interests and subjectivity.

Postscript: What Makes a Good Manager?

All of us have been subordinates. Thus we have all had bosses. Every one of us could probably define what we liked and disliked about the managers we had, enjoyed, or suffered under. Here, for example, are some thoughts on what makes a good boss.

A good boss . . .

. . . *gives employees space.* A manager who constantly looks over employees' shoulders, checking on them, conveys the message "I don't trust you to work, or to work well, if I'm not around." Understandably, most employees resent that message.

On the other hand, relatively few employees are content to work entirely without supervision. People dislike working in a vacuum. They need to know what they are supposed to do and how well they are expected to do it. That means that employees will have periodic conferences with the boss, informal or formal, during which the boss says, in effect, "These are the things we have to accomplish. This is your part of it. These are the standards and the schedules we must observe." Then the manager leaves the employee to do the job, with a degree of control and monitoring that has been explained.

. . . *expects employees to have goals.* The good manager sits down with employees from time to time to make sure they are getting what they want from the work, as far as is possible. Such a manager recognizes that his or her employees have certain needs that can be met through work—and probably nowhere else. But the manager doesn't only *ask* about the employee's needs. He or she tries to make sure they are fulfilled.

. . . *answers the question, "How'm I doing?"* If employees are not working effectively, they need to know that, painful as it is. The work the employee does is probably as important to that employee as it is to the organization. When the employee senses that the work is not going well, he or she experiences tension, which further inhibits good work. So the manager should not delay in criticizing or counseling.

The employee also wants to know when the work has gone well. Employees don't want to be taken for granted. When they feel, inside, that they've done well, they want it reinforced by their managers.

. . . *knows employees want to grow.* People may get much satisfaction from the work they do day to day. But that satisfaction won't last if they continue to do essentially the same work for years. They want to know that in three to five years, say, they will be capable of doing tasks and fulfilling responsibilities that they cannot now. Or, that they'll be able to do what they do now better and easier.

Therefore, it's important for employees to have a manager who asks, "What do you want to do with the rest of your life? Where do you want to go?" In asking those important questions, the manager is showing that the employee is valued.

. . . *makes the job exciting.* Texas entrepreneur H. Ross Perot once said that an employer has an obligation to make a job exciting for employees. It's not that difficult to do. You can make work meaningful to employees by showing them that it is important to the overall work and objectives of the organization. You can help employees to set goals so that they can have a clear sense of achievement. You can assign employees to work that you believe will satisfy personal needs and be significant to them. You can create in employees an expectation of reward: "Do a good job, and it will be recognized."

Results come when people are achieving what is important to them. Motivation is high; productivity follows. When you know how to unblock, to free, to enhance the motivating forces in the people who report to you, you'll enjoy superior performance results.